UNDERSTANDING
TROUT BEHAVIOR

UNDERSTANDING TROUT BEHAVIOR

John Goddard
and
Brian Clarke

THE LYONS PRESS
Guilford, Connecticut
An imprint of The Globe Pequot Press

FRONTISPIECE: *A native New England brook trout.*
Cover photograph by Tim Irwin.

Principal photography by John Goddard.
All other photography by Andy Anderson (page 16), R. Valentine Atkinson (pages
13, 73, 129, 136, 146), Tim Leary (pages 2, 78), and John Randolph (pages 8, 51).

Illustrations by Rod Walinchus.

Printed in the United States of America

10 9 8 7 6 5 4 3

The Library of Congress Cataloging-in-Publication Data is available on file.

CONTENTS

PREFACE

I am writing most of the books in Lefty's Little Library of Fly Fishing. But from time to time, I will be calling upon the services of writer friends of mine who are especially skilled in specialized but important areas of fly fishing to prepare books for us.

This is the first such offering in the Library, a book written by two Englishmen, John Goddard and Brian Clarke, which originally appeared under the title, *The Trout and the Fly — A New Approach*. I consider it a pleasure and an honor that John and Brian have agreed to let me present this material to you in our Library format.

John Goddard, I believe, is the best trout fisherman I have ever spent time on the water with. He has published more than a dozen books on the subject, and is recognized around the world as a true authority. Brian Clarke is also a published fly-fishing writer and a highly respected trout fisherman in his country.

The Trout and the Fly was published in England and the United States in 1980, but sold only a relatively modest number of copies in this country. I regard this as a shame, because that means that few American fly fishermen have had the opportunity to read this fascinating work. For our American readers, I have selected what I feel are the most important portions of the book, and we have reproduced in our edition what I believe you will come to regard as some of the most valuable information in the Library. Certainly any fly fisherman who seriously pursues our most popular freshwater gamefish, the wily trout, will benefit enormously from acquiring the knowledge about the trout's behavior and its viewpoint on the world around it which is set forth so clearly by John and Brian.

I warn you, however, that it will take some serious study to derive all the benefit of the book's numerous insights. So I hope you will take the time to read it carefully. I believe you will enjoy it, and I know it will improve your trout fishing.

Tight lines, but not too tight!

Lefty Kreh
Cockeysville, Maryland
January 13, 1993

OVERLEAF: *A mayfly on England's River Test.*

PROLOGUE:
THE TROUT AND
THE FLY

More books have been written about the trout than about any other fish, and perhaps even any other animal; and more books have been written about fly fishing than about any other branch of the angler's art.

What is it about the trout and the fly that fascinates so?

Certainly, in the case of the trout, it is not his size. There are many fish that grow bigger than he; and anglers, in any event, make few distinctions between trout of different sizes: it is not *absolute* size that is important to the angler; it is — where it is a factor at all — *relative* size: the size of the fish we want or have caught, compared to other fish in the water. A half-pound trout from an upland stream can give every bit as much pleasure in its way, as does a two-pound trout from a rich lowland river, or a five-pound trout from a lake.

If it is not his size, then is it his intelligence? Is the trout endowed with wits beyond his kind? Has he a brain to match our own; to parry and thrust as we plot and scheme?

No, it is hardly his intelligence. The trout is not intelligent, even for a fish. How could he be caught on flies at all, how could he — given his excellent sight — be so terminally indiscriminating, if he were intelligent?

Then what? If it is obviously not his intelligence and his size, then what can it be that allures so? His beauty?

Well, certainly the trout is a beautiful creature. He is exquisitely streamlined; a poem to the eye as he throbs on the current, with the waters sleeking by him like liquid, silent time. And his coloring is spectacular, too, painted by the Master's hand; now gold and olive, now blue and silver, now mottled with red spots and black; the most delicate brushwork on a glistening sheen. So — yes, his beauty must be a factor.

And what else? His fight? Yes, again — certainly his powerful fight. The trout — in particular the trout with a river current to help him — is the most volatile freshwater fish that swims.

That is not to say he is the most dogged, or the most powerful: in England, the carp and the barbel are both stronger than he: but they are not as dashing. And above all, perhaps, they do not leap. They do not break that barrier of the water surface, to show themselves in elemental and outraged beauty, in the manner of the trout. They do not, with that single thrust of the tail, leap not simply into our sight, but like some glistening lance, clearly into the mind in arrested detail.

Who cannot see it now? The line lengthening and lengthening as he nears the surface, and as the reflections above him distort, and then rock. In a shaving off a second, a fragment off time, he is not there and then he is, in lightning slow motion: in cinematographic frames that will play back as dreams long after the summer has gone.

Images. The arch of his body painted on afternoon air; water, drawn up from his tail in a quicksilvered skirt, a membrane mirror stretched beyond the point of pain, and bursting like shattered mosaic; spray, like crystals impaled upon sunbeams. The glimpse of a cocked-white eye, sightless in the impervious air, and the fly, feathered Judas, clicked in the corner of his jaw, with the pink of his mouth inside. And then the crash; the plume of water as he re-enters *his* world, before walking on his tail, down an eddy. Oh yes, the fight and the leap are important factors in the fascination of the trout.

And there is something else. His rise — again, that breaking of the barrier between him and us. The gleam of sunlight on camouflaged flank; magic, ebbing rings. *Pure* magic. They wrench the attention, they magnetize the eye, in a way that the feeding habits of other fishes never do. They draw the mind down into that silent void, pull the mind down into his mysterious, liquid womb.

And it is not just the rise, per se, but the wonderful variety of his rise, as well. The most delicate, subliminal sip: so delicate, sometimes, that it can't have happened, can't have happened, *did* it? And the slash — violent, furious, predatory, a challenge splashed high in the air. And the roll, oiled and languid from broad dark shoulder to sun-shot tail.

Yes, his rise is a factor, too; an important factor. And there are many other considerations, besides: perhaps as many attractions to the trout as there are anglers who fish for him.

Perhaps an even more interesting question, though, is not why the trout should command affection so, but why the *fly*? Why is this curious code embraced? *Why* have such esoteric limitations on the catching of a fish, been handed from father to son, from country to country until now, throughout much of the world, the "only" way to pursue the trout, for millions, is with feathered confections on hooks?

We do not — do we? — impose the code of *imitation* on the pursuit of other fish, as a point of ethics and pride. The world is not populated by men and women who drift floating "bread" of cotton wool, to carp as the light goes down; or by matchmen who lie abed at night devising new dressings of the larva of the bluebottle, with which to deceive their quarry. *They* use the real thing, we *imitate* — with all of the complications which that involves.

Of course, we *do* add to the sport by accepting the fly: and not just in difficulty, either. Fly dressing is almost a pursuit on its own; and for some, fly casting is an interest even where there are no fish.

But it is not these things about the fly, and the problems and diversities which it presents, that make fly fishing the fascination that it is. They may be important for some, but they are effects and not the cause.

There are, like the trout itself no doubt, as many fascinations about the fly as there are men who fish it. At the heart of them all, we believe there are four that are of special importance. The first and the third are considerations that apply to other forms of angling, though in a less direct way; the others are fly fishing's own.

The first consideration, we believe, is that man is a natural hunter, and that fly fishing — particularly fly fishing on rivers — gives him an opportunity to *stalk* his quarry, as he did before memory began. Other branches of angling are hunting, too: but few give the opportunity to hunt *specific* fish. The fly enables the angler to act out, in more than a mannered way, some elemental trace of the forest and glade that lies within us all.

The second reason we suggest, why the fly is so attractive, is that it draws the fish up from his position in the

Landing a brown trout on the South Island of New Zealand. ➤

water, and causes him to make the breathtaking rise that we have already discussed. And in causing his quarry to rise, it enables the angler not simply to deceive it by cunning but to see the moment of deception; to witness the consideration of his skills.

The third consideration is that the moment of the "take" is utterly direct: him there, us here, joined simply by the line and the rod, down into our feeling hands.

We react not to a float that intervenes, nor to the movement of a weight which deadens, but to him, at once. There is nothing at all to dilute the contact. Only the drifted bait compares in other forms of angling; and only the *floated* drifted bait enables the take itself to be seen in a similar way.

And so to the fourth consideration: one that is fly fishing's own; one that concerns "the bait".

One of the reasons that the fly has the following it enjoys, we believe, is because of the very *absence* of "bait". And one of the reasons why men have devoted so many of their energies to solving the problems of the fly is because the problems that the fly presents are *aesthetic* problems: problems that lead immediately to clean, aesthetic solutions or else to more aesthetic problems. Problems (and we write as men who have fished for all manners of fish in all manners of ways, with all manners of bait both dead and alive) that do not involve *mess* in their preparation. There are no buckets of goo and slices of gore; no baskets and bins to burden our approach.

The fly is a physically clean device; one that lends itself to delicacy and mobility. And like us, we believe, other fly fishers are glad of the fact. So the fly, among all its many other blessings, lends *elegance* to the pursuit of trout.

Let us now look at each of the two — at the trout and his fly — more closely.

In the looking, let us remember that we are not setting out to study English trout in English rivers, or American trout in American rivers, or New Zealand's trout in New Zealand's rivers. While circumstances may change in the specific — for example the river may be clearer or more opaque, or be wider or deeper — the basic facts with which we are concerned, have a common denominator from which all else flows; and it is that common denominator with which we are here concerned.

A trout is a trout is a trout; and his life is governed by the same series of needs and laws, *wherever he swims.*

OVERLEAF:*Angler enjoying the day on a private spring creek.*

PART ONE

OBSERVATION: MAN AND TROUT

HOW TO SEE TROUT

In setting out to observe the trout, two related points need to be borne in mind. The first is that he is not going to be easy to see; the second is that given reasonable light, clarity of water, and a little knowledge and effort, he *can* be seen.

We should not be surprised that seeing the trout in his own environment is not going to be an easy business. The trout has not evolved to make himself easy to see, for predators on wing, fin or feet. He has evolved to make himself difficult to see; and the fact that he has survived so long, and is so widely distributed, is eloquent testimony to his success.

In the proving grounds of evolution, he has learned all manner of tricks to make himself difficult to see. He is, for example, not simply born with a coloration which marries him to his native river: he will change color (and has been observed to make the change in a matter of days) to take on the appropriately camouflaging hues, when transferred to a different water.

More specifically, the trout often adopts a camouflage custom-designed to a specific reach *and even lie*.

If a trout frequents a beat lined with bright gravel and sand, he may gleam like morning gold. If he inhabits the deeper water, or a pool that has long been silled up, he will be many shades darker on the back. If he inhabits the crisp, fresh-laundered runs between weedbeds on alkaline streams, he will often be bright silver, like the sea trout. Brian Clarke has seen a number of trout on heavily weeded streams that had heavy pigmentations of olive green. John Goddard has even seen trout with dark, vertical, perch-like stripes on their sides as a direct result, he believes, of living in close proximity to reeds growing up through the water.

So there are no grounds at all for expecting the trout to be easy to see.

But that does not mean we need eyes like lasers, in order to see him. We know men of technically modest sight, who see more fish than most; and G.E.M. Skues it is comforting to note, saw well enough into the water with a single eye, to found an entirely new branch of the visual, fly-fishing arts.*

It is our experience that in the matter of seeing the trout in his element, it is not eyesight that transcends all else. The ability to spot the trout consistently, hinges upon several factors. The first is knowing how to make the best use of what eyesight we have been given — *how* to look; the second lies in knowing *what* to look for; and the third, in knowing *where* to look.

In this chapter, and those that immediately follow it, we will look at each of these factors in turn. But before we do, let us raise a fourth consideration; *practice*. Practice in seeing fish — particularly practice with a companion who himself knows how to see them — is very important

*Nymph fishing — *Editor.*

indeed. It will enable you to improve your powers of observation, no matter what stage they might hitherto have reached.

The Eyes

Few fishermen (or indeed, anyone else) give much thought to the most important consideration in seeing anything: the amount of light which reaches the eyes.

In looking for the trout in his environment, we are going to be looking for very subtle indications indeed that he is present. For this reason, we need to admit to the eye as much of the important light (which is to say, light from the water area into which we are looking) as we can; and conversely, we need to cut off from the eye as much unimportant light (light from areas into which we are not looking) as we are able.

The first significant physical aid we can give our eyes, that will enable them to perform their critical role better, will be something to cut out the glare of the sky. One way that this can be achieved, is by the simple expedient of wearing a wide-brimmed or long-peaked hat; another is the use of a linen-backed eyeshade of the type used by some tennis players, golfers, and spectators of outdoor sports. The second physical help we can give to the eyes is a pair of polarized glasses to reduce surface reflections. Because all reflections manage to do — as we shall discuss in a moment — is to prevent the eye from piercing the surface film.

In choosing your polarized glasses, do not make the mistake of trying to combine "sunglasses" with "seeing" glasses. Sunglasses have no place in "seeing" fishing. They simply reduce the amount of light coming to the eye: and it is light — light from the water in which the fish reside — that you want.

*Buy the clearest polarized glasses you can find.**

You can, incidentally, improve the usefulness of polarized glasses on a given stretch of water, by rotating them slightly on your nose. In one position they'll cut out one plane of light, enabling you to see into one part of the river; in another position, they'll cut out other areas of reflection, and enable you to see down into new water. (Of such fine dodges as these are successful fishermen made!)

Using the Light

The most favorable conditions for seeing into the water occur on windless days when the sun is either behind the shoulders or immediately overhead.

Conversely, the worst conditions occur in high winds, when the surface becomes rippled, and on cloudy days, when the surface throws back a uniform, impenetrable gray. When there is a ripple, it becomes impossible to see into the water at all. In conditions of much cloud, the only real hope of seeing into the water is by gaining a vantage point high above the surface. For this reason, on these occasions, maximum use should be made of high banks with cover behind them; and of rocks, logs and other bankside furniture which can be stood upon to give a higher perspective, when there is cover behind.

On the sunny day, few problems are likely to be presented from late morning until early afternoon. Depend-

---

*It is a small point but if you are shopping for polarized lenses, and you're not sure that those on the counter have been so treated — simply hold one pair of glasses in front of another, and rotate them in opposite directions. If, in looking through one to the other, the lenses appear to go dark, then they're both polarized. If they do not appear to go dark, then at least one set of lenses is not polarized.

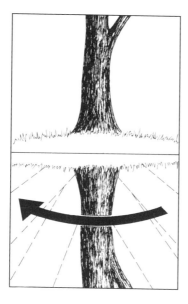

How the reflection of a tree (or any other large object on the opposite bank) can cut out the surface glare and enable the fly fisherman to see down into the water, as he walks along the bank.

ing, however, upon the time of year and the bank being fished, there is unlikely to be some time when the sun is not ahead of you, and the water has not taken on its silvered sheen.

When it does, there are several things that you can do, to alleviate the problem.

The first, of course, is again to take advantage of the bankside furniture, to gain a higher perspective: at least that way you will gain some insight to the water under your own bank.

A second and more comprehensive approach is to seek out, if it is available to you, a stretch of river that is lined on the far bank with trees: their reflections will remove the sheen, and enable you to see down through the surface without trouble.

A third measure you can employ, if the banks are mostly open, is to seek out a single tree or bush on the opposite bank, and glue your eyes to its reflection, as slowly you walk your own side of the river. Again, its single reflection will cut out the glare and will follow you around, as you move. In effect, it gives you a moving vertical line that is reflection-free, enabling you to scan the water little by little.

Movement and Concentration

When, either because the day is right or you have adopted one of the ploys above, you are in a position from which you can see into the water — stand still. Water cannot be scanned thoroughly when you are on the move at the trot.

As you move, so your perspective on objects changes; as you move, so they change shape; as you move, so they move in relation to other objects which may themselves (for example, weedbeds) be moving. And in looking for all the subtleties of light, and shape, and movement that the camouflaged trout is going to present to us, it makes no sense to volunteer for handicaps.

So — stand still, and concentrate. Do not concentrate *on* the water, concentrate on a depth and an area *in* the water. And bring your willpower into play. Resolve that if fish are there, then you will see them: like so much else in life, seeing fish if they are there to be seen at all, is an attitude of mind.

If experience tells you that the stretch of water you are looking at is "holding" water, and you see one fish, do not rest your investigation there. The odds are that if the water looks good, and it can be seen to hold one trout, then it will hold others. Look for the rest before you resort to any kind of action: the one you haven't seen will be the one you spook; and by that quaint angling law that we know so well, it will be the biggest of the bunch, as well.

And there is something else. Remember the effect of light upon the eye. If you've gone to the trouble of wearing an eyeshade or a hat to allow your pupils to open and admit more light, do not waste the advantage which that gives you. Do not, for example, range your eyes from dark, to light, to dark. All that you'll achieve will be to cause the pupils to contract when you look at the light and cause them to stay temporarily contracted when they look back at the dark.

As a result, very little will have been gained from your hat or your eyeshade; and very little will have been seen, as well. *When looking for trout, address the shaded areas first, and then address the areas of light.*

And when you move from areas of light to areas of dark, give your eyes time to adjust.

What to Look For (General)

Knowing what to look for, is the Catch 22 of seeing fish: you're lucky if you see fish without knowing what to look for; but you don't really know what to look for, until you've learned to recognize fish.

Of course, if that were literally and absolutely true, dictionaries would lose much of their value as aids to spelling. We could not pick up a dictionary to check the spelling of a word, because to look the word up in a book arranged in alphabetical order, we would first need to know the sequence in which the letters occurred.

But just as we manage with dictionaries, so we can manage with trout, given some determination, common sense, and sensitivity.

The question of seeing trout can be likened to the principles of "computer matching". With a little experience, we can imprint upon the mind's eye what we might expect to see; and when the picture recorded by the eyes matches the image imprinted upon the mind, then the brain registers "fish!"

The analogy encapsulates perfectly the problem of those who set out to find fish, and fail to see them even when fish are there. They have imprinted upon their minds the images of fish, and then gone off in search of a visual image to match their mental image.

Almost the *last* thing that the experienced observer looks for is a fish — or at least a *whole* fish. He looks for parts of fish, indications of fish, hints of fish, winks and suggestions of fish, as set out below.

As will become clear shortly one of the most common indications of a trout is its tail: not the whole fish, not the rear half of the fish; not even the shape of a clearly defined tail; simply the throbbing, rhythmic shadow that the tail suggests, pulsing in the water.

The experienced man will have "tail rhythms" clearly fixed among his mental images; and when his eyes see that metronome's shadow, his brain registers "tail" and then the "fish!" bell rings. When the inexperienced man has a mental image of a fish — or even a tail as he is accustomed to seeing it — and his eyes arrive at that throbbing shade, his brain does not register a match, and he does not perceive the trout.

Frank Sawyer, in his historic book *Nymphs and the Trout*, gives a graphic illustration of the mind of a master observer at work; and the clearest demonstration of the matching process.

Sawyer recalls that often when he has been looking for pike to trap, he has failed to see trout, even though they have been lying in open positions; and conversely, that when he has been seeking trout, he has failed to see pike.

In the case of Sawyer his mental image was so refined that he wasn't looking for a visual match to hints of a mental "fish", he was looking for a visual match to hints of a mental species of fish. Very few anglers indeed, reach that degree of sophistication!

What to Look For (Specific)

Physical clues to the presence of fish fall into two broad and often overlapping categories: movements; and shadows and shapes. Before setting out to perceive them, there is one essential preparation: to "read yourself into" each stretch of water, as you come to it.

Every reach of every river has its own features: weedbeds, large rocks, undulating pebble banks, gullies, buckets, shallows and deeps; and each has its own character too; a "personality" that is the product of some or all of these features, and the current's reaction to them. Study this "character" of the water, first, and understand what you can expect to see. There is no magic involved: the current and the riverbed furniture show what you can expect to see: it is what is there.

When the pattern of events, the interplays of light and contortions of the current, are clearly imprinted upon your mind begin, then, to look for *anything different or foreign*; anything out of place; anything that draws the eye twice to any piece of water as it presents itself.

In looking for the foreign and the unusual, have imprinted upon your mind, the following.

Movements

The greatest betrayer of prey to predator is movement. Camouflage — as we have already discovered — is a magnificent device that is found everywhere in the animal kingdom. It is designed to merge an otherwise naked creature into its background. But backgrounds do not move; or at least, they do not transport themselves from one place to another, even though elements of them may bend and sway in response to winds and currents.

It is because backgrounds do not physically transport themselves that camouflaged creatures, almost without exception, "freeze" when danger approaches. The very absence of flight is a protective mechanism.

The protection goes when movement begins, as any stooping hawk or hunting cat will tell you.

And so it is with the trout. Perhaps the most common factor that betrays the trout is its movement. So imprint this upon your mind: *movement equals fish.*

There are many kinds of movement. Perhaps the most common of all the giveaways, as we have already discussed, is the pulse of the trout's tail, in the current: a throbbing shadow with (sometimes) a clean, vertical, trailing edge.

It is extraordinary that one can see the pulse of the tail, without being able to see the whole fish first; but be assured that it is so. Be assured, as well, that this is the essence of "matching".

A second kind of movement to be alert for is a flash of light from below water, caused by the abrupt turn of a fish and the reflection of the sunlight from its flank. Yet another signal is the blink of white from the mouth of a trout, as it takes a nymph. It may sound unbelievable that such a tiny movement can be seen — but we assure you that it is so.

A third type of telltale movement is the one that is, for want of a better term, "out of synch" with the other movements we can see or expect to see in the river.

The push of a tail, a leisurely realignment, and a nymph disappears. The split-second blink of white as the trout opens his mouth is one of the most important clues that the observant nymph fisherman looks for, in helping him to pinpoint his quarry.

Give or take the odd eddy and whirl, the movement of the water is downstream; and everything that is floating free in the water, or is growing up into it from the bottom, reflects the fact. So look for:

1) Anything which suggests movement upstream, against the current;

2) Anything which drops downstream in a controlled way; or which drops downstream and then stops;

3) Anything which is moving in one direction, when the current is rhythmically wafting weed in another;

4) Anything which appears to drift from one weedbed to another, and does not move back again in harmony with the movements of the vegetation.

It is worth stressing again that you are not looking for a fish shape doing these things: you are looking for anything at all doing these things: it may be a dark shadow, it may be a light reflection; it may be something light *and* dark, or something dark upon dark or light upon light. It is any kind of foreign movement, that you are looking for.

Do not always expect to see something physical moving *in* the water. Look for changes in the movement of the water itself. Again, the movement of the current is in a downstream direction; and a moment or two spent in observation of the surface convolutions of the water will show what the eye can reasonably expect to perceive. When that "normal" base of information has been stored in the mind, look a minute or two longer. Very often, it will be possible to see momentary additional changes of the water surface, as the current reacts to the movement of an unseen fish.

In rippled water* look for a local patch of ripple in which the wavelets move broadside to the general current. In smooth water look for regularly shaped reflections that become irregular and for sharp reflections that suddenly blur. Imprint all of these phenomena upon your mind, and imprint "fish!" upon your mind, beside them.

Shadows and Shapes

Shadows are an important register in the mental gallery of the fish watcher. They come in all kinds, and bear all manner of significance. Two are worth a special mention, because they introduce the need for caution.

The first — and one of the most difficult to see — is that produced by a fish lying in deep water; in particular, by the fish lying in a deep bucket, in the middle of a shallow reach.

The trout that lies in a deep pool spends most of his time close to the bottom, because it is safer there. He will be a shadow upon a shadow; or just occasionally, if he is newly arrived, a marginally lighter shade than that of the dark bottom upon which he lies.

---

*See pages 58-59, *Locating Invisible Fish*.

The camouflage of some trout is so perfectly matched to their surroundings that only the most practiced and penetrating eyes will pick them out. In this photograph there is a large trout lying in a slight depression or bucket in this shallow stretch of water.

If such a fish sees you before you see him, you may spend fruitless minutes trying to do him wrong. Such a fish will not bolt when he is alarmed: he will simply sink deeper down onto the bottom, pressing himself almost upon it; putting as much distance between you and his good self, as he can. He knows you are there; he knows you know he is there. It is stalemate. You must approach the water with caution.

The second shadow that is worth special mention occurs on graveled bottoms, in shallower water, on sunny days. It is a shadow, for once, that looks quite like a fish.

Never cast to a shadow such as this, in the conditions described, without careful observation, first. You may, of course, cast if you wish; but often enough you'll be there till Doomsday and some way beyond, before you come near to inducing a take.

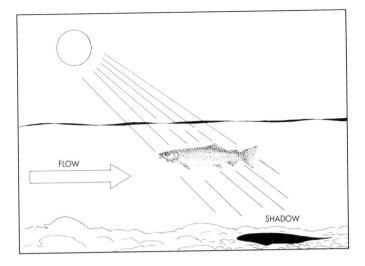

How a shadow on the bottom can reveal the true position of a fish lying elsewhere. In bright sunlight, draw a mental line through the water between the shadow on the bottom, and the sun. The fish that you are seeking, will lie somewhere along that line.

The reason is that this shade is often not a fish at all, but a genuine shadow: and the fish that is creating it is some distance away. To find the fish itself, draw a mental line through the water, from the shadow towards the sun. The trout you are seeking, will lie some distance from the bottom, somewhere along that line.

Do not expect a fish such as we have just described to be easy to see. Fish that lie in mid-water can be very difficult to see. Indeed, perhaps the most difficult fish of all to see, is one that rides close to the surface, over a graveled bottom, in briskly flowing, eddying water.

It is one that Brian Clarke has come to term the "see-through" fish; and which John Goddard refers to with equal validity, as "the shimmer". It is a mid-water fish that is characterized by the subtleties of light which play upon it; and not, as in the case of our previous friend, by the light it cuts off the bottom.

The see-through fish is at his most transparent, on sunny days. The sunlight melts as it passes through the rumpling, rippling surface, and splashes fluidly down his sleek and mobile form; it reflects off the brilliance of his scales, oils down his back, drips off his fins. It dissolves him utterly; and he evaporates into the light, the water and the stones around him.

When you have come to see the see-through fish, you will be seeing most of the trout in the river.

There are two kinds of *line* that betray the trout, as well. The first is on the tail that we have already mentioned: the vertical trailing edge. It is the most common betrayer of the trout which lies with his head under a weedbed. Presumably he feels safe once the darkness of the fronds closes about his eyes; but like the ostrich that buries his head in the sand he leaves, as it were, something behind.

The see-through fish: a trout that rides high in rippled water on sunny days, can almost evaporate before the eyes.

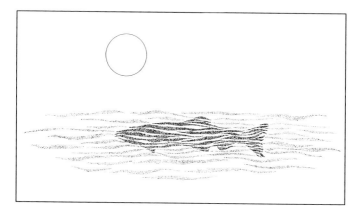

It is surprising how many trout leave their tails protruding: and it is the vertical edge which gives them away, contrasting sharply with the horizontal wafting of the weed alongside.

The other kind of line that should be framed in your mental gallery is the thin, straight line that runs due upstream/downstream. This line is at its most noticeable (and when that is said, it is not saying much) on clear gravel reaches which have few distinguishing features.

It is most easily seen from broadside-on; and for this and other reasons it pays not simply to fix the eyes on the water ahead but on the water opposite, too.

The straight line that runs upstream/downstream is very often a trout: a fish whose darker back can just barely be seen, but whose sides reflect the light and riverbed, and all but disappear.

WHERE TROUT LIE

However big he is, and whatever kind of water he inhabits, the trout is an expert at survival: in knowing where the food is, and getting it; and in conserving his energies and keeping out of trouble, when he is not.

But places good for eating in, and places good for surviving in, are by no means necessarily the same: a fact that the fish himself learns at a very early age, if he is to learn at all. As a consequence, it is not possible to say that a fish has "his lie" and so to suggest that the trout has one spot and only one spot, where we can expect to find him on a river.

Some trout *do* have only one lie, but many more have two, three or several at any one time and, over the course of a year, perhaps a dozen or more, as they accommodate themselves to changes in water levels, the appearance and disappearance of obstacles and features on the riverbed, and to the availability and otherwise of different forms of insect food as the season progresses. For this reason it similarly is not sensible to assume that a fish has been caught because it is not where we have seen it on occasions before. It may have "gone", but it may not have gone permanently or even very far.

Because, as anglers, we are concerned with *feeding* fish, let us consider the needs of the feeding trout, in modest detail. Only by understanding something of his needs will we come to understand (and to exploit) his behavior.

The principal need of the trout that wants to eat, is food. Much of the food which the trout eats on rivers (although by no means all of it) appears all at once, as it were: typically as in migrations of nymphs and hatches of fly. And it is the sudden appearance of substantial amounts of food, that is the probable trigger of his general feeding response.

The trout soon discovers that tiny, vulnerable creatures like flies and nymphs are at the mercies of the currents, and tend to get concentrated into channels created by the water and its reaction to obstacles to its progress: to impediments like weeds, and stones, and piling and bridge supports. And not unnaturally, the trout positions himself to take advantage of the most concentrated flows.

These concentrations do not, of course, occur only at the surface. It is possible for the surface current to be taking floating flies in one direction while a local sub-surface current, created by the reaction of the water to some sub-surface obstacle, takes nymphs in a different direction.

This is a typical circumstance when a single trout may have two or three feeding locations, at any one time of the year — quite apart from the "survival" or "resting" lie

Not all fish become "preoccupied" with food close to the surface. This trout has adopted the characteristic attitude of a fish hunting on the bottom for caddis larvae, stonefly nymphs, shrimps and the like.

which provides him with the security he needs while staying out of trouble, and conserving his strength. One position may be favored when the food is on, in or immediately beneath the surface film; a second position may be preferred when it is necessary to lie close to the bottom, to acquire what food is on offer. A typical third position would not be a fixed point at all, but a whole area or beat of the water which the trout will patrol when actively hunting food from the riverbed: food like shrimps and caddis larvae, which the current may not naturally bring to his palate.

Once he has found a lie, he will prove tenacious and difficult to shift. He will leave if he is driven away by an angler or a bigger fish; or sometimes if a pike takes up residence nearby. But otherwise — at least if he is a brown trout — he will stay. He will display real aggression to other trout that encroach upon his territory, and even if driven away by predators will return as quickly as he can, when the danger has passed.

It is by no means the case that because their basic needs are the same, the trout feeding in the faster and shallower reach leads a similar existence to that of his friend in the slower beat, elsewhere. The two, in their different kinds of lies, lead very different lives.

In fast water, the current brings food down to the trout at a hasty rate: there is a vague shape ahead of him in the stream one moment, it is beside him the next, and being whirled away the second after that. If he is to eat whatever it is that approaches, his decision must be made quickly, and executed just as fast. There is no time for "Oh-dear-me", and "Shall-I-or-shan't-I?" It's now or never, grab or not. So the trout in fast water is a vulnerable trout, for that reason alone: if he grabs, and grabs the wrong fly, he's done for.

But that is not all.

As we shall see in greater detail where we deal with vision, the trout's view of the outside world is not only not very wide (because in shallow water he is by definition nearer the surface, and so has a smaller window): it is often desperately distorted, too.

Water that rushes over the riverbed cannot dictate its course. It must follow the contour of the bed: a bed gouged and riddled, humped and gnarled. Each distortion of the bottom contorts the water flowing over it, creating a variety of whirls and vortices, whirlpools and wrinkles, that pucker and pleat the surface film. And it is through all of this that the trout must see, and hope to discern the true from the false.

The trout that lies in fast, shallow water to feed is a mettlesome fish indeed. But he leads a dangerous existence, and not always a long one consequently. Few big trout indeed reside in the shallows, before the urge to mate takes its hold.

The trout that feeds in slower and deeper water leads a very different life. There is no darting this way and that for him; no extrovert and suicidal lunge.

He hangs around mid-water; perhaps a little above, perhaps a little below. He can see above, below, to the sides and ahead. His food — unless he lifts some larvae from the bottom, or rummages for shrimps amid the weed — arrives in conspicuous and stately procession.

He can see it approaching from a long way off: and not in single, tiny morsels that must be concentrated upon intently lest some fluke of the current sweeps them away, but in tens and dozens and hundreds from which he can take his pick.

The trout in slower, deeper water is a choosy trout when he wants to be: he has all the time in the world to scrutinize, if he cares to take it — and quite often he does.

Lies — Specific

As we have indicated elsewhere, exactly which lie the trout chooses on a particular day will be influenced by many factors: by his size, and the range of options physically open to him; by the time of year; by the height of the water; by the direction and strength of the wind; and by many other factors including, not least, the kind of food his beat supports.

Few lies are satisfactory in all conditions, providing not only food when it is wanted, but security (which means an amenable current, and protection from predators) when it isn't; and those that are, are contested vigorously by the fish.

That, of course, is the reason why lies that are obviously "good" as defined above *hold* big fish, and often aggressive fish: fish, in other words, that are capable of fighting off incursions by their lesser brethren.

In the list of typical lies and holding places which follows, only two or three fall into the year-round category. In *every* case, however, where the lie is a feeding lie, there will by definition be a supply of food: and almost always a narrower band of current, a channel or an eddy to concentrate it further.

When looking for the most likely lies on any stretch of any river, look in the first instance for concentrations in the principal line of the river's current (for example, where the weight of water pushes into the *outside* of the bend); and in the second instance, look for eddies of the principal current.

And so to specific lies.

Bridges

Any fisherman with more than a morning's experience knows that the water beneath a bridge is a likely lie for a trout; and often, for a big trout. It is that rare phenomenon, the "complete" lie.

It is not difficult to see why. A bridge is usually cited on the narrowest section of river compatible with its main purpose. And the narrower a section of the river is, the deeper it will be: in the absence of Moses, the water cannot rise up; it must dip down by carving away the bottom. So the water beneath the average bridge tends to be deeper than the norm; and if the bridge has arches, the bottom becomes more deeply sculpted still, where the current is deflected from the sides and supports.

As a result, all the food borne by the river is not channeled into a narrow thrust of water where the banks close in: it is deflected into secondary, even tighter channels.

If you can see under the arch of the bridge, look first at the point, below the upstream side, at which the thrusts of current shrugged off by the structures converge.

Riding the deep, dark water beneath the bridge, ready to sink softly out of sight.

Most of the river's drifting food will be funneled into that point, and the trout will be waiting there, with jaws agape. If no fish is apparent there — look then along the *sides* of the bridge, whence the food will have been carried by the back eddy.

(Bridges, marvelous constructions though they often are, have two disadvantages that every angler knows. There are unwritten laws — indeed, so consistently do they manifest themselves that they probably *are* written; and enshrined, it may further be surmised, in finest copperplate — about bridges and the fish which lie beneath them. The first is that the lower the bridge is and the more difficult it is to cast beneath, the larger any trout will be. If it is utterly impossible to cast beneath a bridge, then there a granddaddy will lie. The second law states that a wind will blow in any direction *other* than upstream, under a bridge!)

Hatch Pools

If there is one place where a big fish will be found — a place even more likely than a low bridge to be attractive to the granddaddy of the stream — then it is the hatch pool.

Because of the immense weight of water pouring down on it from the gate above, the hatch pool is always an area of deep water; water, sometimes, to be measured in the tens of feet. And because of the fall, it is well oxygenated, even in the hottest weather.

Look, first, for any sandbanks or gravel banks that might have been built up from the bed. Pay particular attention to the head of such a bank, and to the sides.

Expect the fish, too, to lie in the eddies (of course!) just off the main current; and (of course!) tight into the banks where the current bites.

The blink of the camera shutter catches a trout just below the surface, in the back eddy of a waterfall — and in so doing, makes the presence of the fish appear much more obvious than it otherwise would have been. When the water is in motion, and the surface reflection is changing constantly, trout can be very difficult to see.

Look, too, towards the tail of the pool, where the floor begins to shelve up and the water becomes a glassy glide: fish will often fall back to such a position in the evening; and in the daytime too, if there is a heavy hatch of fly.

Look *on top of the hatch.* It is common for a fish to lie immediately in front of the lip, where the torrent pours down into the pool below, apparently holding station by miraculous powers; almost immobile save for a gentle drift of an inch or two, to either side.

In fact, of course, no fish could live in the full force of the current that forges through the hatch itself and the trout, very sensibly, lies a fraction below the lip where the current is all but negligible; or hangs poised on the cushion of current that pushes back upstream, where the water bounces off the hatch support.

The position at the top of the hatch is a marvelous lie for a fish. But be warned on two counts. He will usually be a nervous, wary fish, that will be difficult to approach; and if you hook him, he'll like as not turn downstream, over the fall and into the pool below.

(Such a trout can be fun. John Goddard remembers a particularly sophisticated and frustrating fish. The trout lay on top of a hatch for several years, and grew big and wise. The pool below his hatch was — unusually — safe for bathing in; and so was much used by local youths for that unreasonable pursuit. To get to the pool, a footbridge across the top of the hatch had to be used. As a consequence, the fish grew very accustomed to human traffic, and its significance. A man who crossed the bridge immediately behind the trout with a towel under his arm, prompted not a flicker of interest. A man who danced upon the footbridge and waved his arms like a windmill in order to frighten the fish, would have collapsed with exhaustion without succeeding. But whenever, year upon year, John Goddard poked the end of a rod stealthily over the bankside to attempt something unspeakable, the trout departed amid an indignant cloud of silt!)

Sills and Weirs

All that has been said about the fish lying on top of the hatch pool applies to the trout that lies on the top of a sill or weir,* with the qualification that the river is not always narrow at such a point, and so the flow of food is less concentrated.

It is by no means uncommon to find a line of fish in position in the glassy water at the immediate upstream edge of the fall.

Because the food is no more concentrated there than it is in the body of the river, it is our belief that such fish have taken up positions there for reasons of physical comfort: because the current, the temperature and the oxygen content of the water itself are more agreeable to the fish that have assumed them than they are in the other lies available to those fish, at that time, elsewhere.

Overhanging Trees

Trees that grow up from the water's edge provide for many of the needs of trout, simply by being there. For example, they provide him with physical cover, which helps to protect him from predators, from the direct heat of the sun, and from the full glare of the light. And, of course, they are the scene of much insect activity and life, so providing the occasional supplementary meal. So any tree which hangs over the river, starts off with a plus.

But there are some trees that mark the lies of fish with all the certainty of a finger from the clouds (though you're

---

*In American usage, threshold or dam — *Editor.*

unlikely to see that, Polaroids or no). These are the trees that hang over deeper pools at the ends of shallows, and under which the current cuts.

Add to such embellishments a breeze that pushes floating flies into the bank beneath the tree, then there's a good chance that any fish there will be a rising fish.

In circumstances such as these (and, when they occur, under tussocks of grass that grow up from the edge of the bank) do not look for your fish in the general direction of the overhanging fronds: the fish, if the current and the wind penetrate that far, will lie so close to the bank as almost to touch it. A foot or 18 inches out can be too far.

Rocks and Other Impediments

Almost every book we have read has drawn attention to the importance of rocks, logs and the like on the riverbed, which act as impediments to the progress of the water. And almost without fail, these books have urged the reader to concentrate his attentions on the downstream side of such obstacles, "where the trout lie in wait for the food".

This is one of those pieces of advice that while sometimes helpful, more often is not.

It is perfectly true that trout often lie in wait for food on the inside edges of eddies which such obstacles often create, on their downstream sides.

But far more often except in very fast water — the trout lie *in front* of rocks, and to the sides of them. And the man who has concentrated his attention *behind* such things has been missing at least half of the fish on offer. And if, hitherto, he has been a wet-fly man fishing down and across, carefully allowing his flies to swing behind the obstacle from his upstream position, he has been lining a high proportion of fish in the river.

A gray shade holding station in a typical lie — ahead of an obstruction rising from the riverbed.

The trout likes the upstream sides of rocks, logs, and goodness-knows-not-what other solid objects that may from time to time appear, for exactly the same reasons that he likes the tops of hatches: because he has a splendid view of what the current is bringing him; and yet is cushioned from the weight of the water.

(But note that there is one exception to all of this. The American cutthroat trout prefers to lie *downstream* of obstacles, almost regardless of the pace of the water. Though with a name like that, he can be forgiven for almost any aberration.)

Weedbeds

A useful rule of thumb for the fly fisherman wanting to find the trout in his river would be, "where there is weed, there are fish".

Weed provides the trout with cover. It harbors the food that he needs in order to live — often in dense concentrations. And, of course, it provides him with places to lie: in the calmer water at the head of the weedbed, where the roots form an obstruction to the flow; and beneath it and downstream of it where the constant sweeping to and fro has eroded channels and dips in the bed.

Look, also, at the top of two distinct weedbeds that emerge side by side from the bottom. The current that each root-hold shrugs off must find a way between them: and so must the food that the current carries. The trout knows it, just as surely as he knows it under bridges, where the same thing occurs.

Pockets and Channels

The trout will take up a position that the inexperienced angler will dismiss at a glance. Often, such a position will occur on broad and apparently featureless shallows.

We all know shallows like this. They occur below rapids, and below the glides where deep pools run off. The river is unusually wide. When the sun is behind the back or overhead, every pebble, every fish, every *caddis*, can be taken in, and it is clear that there is nothing there.

Or is there? The real answer is "yes — trout". The reason why they are there is because we got the premise wrong. The bottom is not featureless. It has small pockets in it, in which trout lie. It has channels in the riverbed, up which trout patrol. Not deep pockets, or deep channels; simply depressions. Where, typically, the average depth across the flats is a foot or so, the depression may be 18 inches; where the average depth is six inches, a channel may be a foot deep.

Such features are very difficult to see. The experienced observer of fish will see the trout before he sees the pocket or channel. Sometimes they will only be discovered by accident, while wading. It is a rare flat that possesses no features at all.

Silt on the Current

There are two valuable clues to lies that are provided by silt suspended on the current.

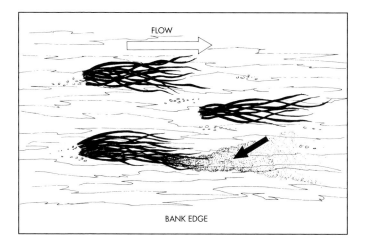

Among the minor but important clues the observant angler will recognize, is a puff of silt drifting down on the current. Sometimes it will have been created by a fish that has seen him, and bolted; sometimes it will betray a fish lying some way upstream that is rummaging among the weeds for nymphs.

The most common cause of silt on the current is a fish that you will not catch. Not yet, that is. This fish lies well down, close to the bottom. He has a splendid view through his big, wide window; and an excellent chance of seeing you, before you see him.

When he *does* see you, he departs. The powerful thrust of his body sends up a cloud of silt from the bottom, that quickly attracts the eye.

In the case of this fish, simply make an accurate mental note of his position, and move on. Next time you're on his territory you'll approach more cautiously, and know exactly where to look.

The other clue that silt can provide can be capitalized upon, at once. It manifests itself merely as a slight graying of the water, in a narrow stream, in an otherwise crystal-line river.

It is a forewarning and not, this time, a sign that your fish has gone.

Thin, constant streams of silt on the current are often caused by fish some distance upstream, rummaging among the weeds for nymphs; or fish that are twisting onto their sides to pick shrimps from tight on the bottom.*

Whenever such a clue is seen it is a signal first to move cautiously, then to look hard, and often to reach for your weighted patterns.

THE LIGHT PATCH

There is one phenomenon concerning the lies of fish in some rivers that is of such great importance that we feel we should address it separately.

It is a subject upon which, at the time of writing, neither of us has seen anything written, anywhere: and yet it provides an instantaneous key to the location of large numbers of trout, in those bodies of water on which the phenomenon occurs.

It has, we believe, a revolutionary significance not only in the pursuit of trout, but in the hunting of other territorial fish, too; and not just on alkaline rivers, but on any river in which there occurs mild algal growth on the bottom; trace growths of filamentous weeds on the bottom; or mild depositions of silt on slow reaches, or on other reaches in periods of low water or drought.

We have termed this phenomenon, with stunning lack of imagination, "the light patch".

---

*See page 61, *Locating Invisible Fish*.

A remarkable observation we have made is the way that large trout on some rivers clean or disturb small areas of the riverbed as a result of constant contact with their bodies, and the steady sweeping of their tails. This photograph clearly illustrates the points we make regarding this phenomenon of the light patch.

The light patch is simply a small area of the riverbed that is marginally lighter in color than the riverbed around. It is caused by a fish of some size holding its position in the current, tight on the bottom: and by the continuous wafting from side to side of his tail.

As the tail pulses softly in the current twice or thrice each second, for hours, days and weeks, the tiny turbulence it creates and the fish's occasional physical contact with the bottom, brushes off any slight deposit or growth of vegetable matter, and simply cleans the stones and bottom beneath. On some chalkstreams the exposed bed, cleaned of debris, can gleam like a heliograph. It is a circumstance which we have witnessed on countless occasions; and when we have removed a trout from a particularly well-marked spot, the lower edge of his tail fin has occasionally shown signs of considerable wear.

In documenting this phenomenon, it should not be taken that we are implying that *all* light patches on the bottom of a stream are caused by the fish themselves. Clearly, that would be nonsense. Many light patches are caused by freakish turbulence in the current, where it curls behind stones and the like. But sufficient numbers *are* caused by fish, to justify closer scrutiny of all light patches on the riverbed than is accorded to any of the more obvious potential lies that we have discussed so far.

Nor, it should be noted, are we suggesting that all fish are capable of leaving their marks in this way, when they lie for a period of time, on the bottom. Very small fish are not, in our experience, capable of creating sufficient turbulence (though, certainly, a *shoal* of small coarse fish is).

Nor are we suggesting that every river provides the conditions in which even a large fish will leave his mark: in particular, the clean-scoured bottom of the upland spate river — even one artificially stocked with larger fish — would not do so. But many rivers already do; and as pollution spreads, and algal growths spread with it, more may yet do so.

Where conditions are ideal — and we have observed light patches caused by fish on many rivers — the change of color denoted by a patch can often be sufficiently dramatic to be visible fifty yards away. *Fifty yards away*. Imagine being able to pinpoint a fish on the bottom, within inches, at such a great distance. As a marker, it is more valuable even than a rise-form, because the rise-form drifts back with the current, and the light patch does not.

Consider, if you will, how many times you have observed "patches of gravel" on a stony bottom, or "patches of sand" on a gravel bottom; or places where the chalk "has come right to the surface". Consider how many times you can recall seeing fish in such places, or near them.

There was no coincidence about that proximity: the fish were showing you where they lived.

So common are light patches, in rivers or areas of rivers that have light algal or weed growth on the bottom, or filmy deposits of silt, that broad shallows can look as though they have been waded across in studded boots, by a stumbling giant.

But the light patch is invaluable in looking for trout in deep water, too. It glows from the bottom like a beacon in the night. Not with that intensity, of course, but with that significance, once its causes have been understood.

Even if you do not see a trout on a light patch (and, because he may have several lies, you may well not) do not be in too much of a hurry to move on. He *may*, of course, have been caught. But it is every bit as common for a trout to lie a foot upstream of the light patch, as it is for him to lie directly upon it.

If a fish is not immediately apparent, look for the fanning of his tail at the upstream edge of the patch. It is his tail that causes most of the erosion, as explained a moment ago: and most erosion occurs just behind him, because that is where the current carries the turbulence he creates.

(Note, too, that in very shallow water, an unoccupied light patch may well mark an evening lie. Shallow-water lies are often only occupied by fish under the cover of darkness — in part, no doubt, because the trout feels less vulnerable then.)

Communal Lies

Discovery of the significance of the light patch has led us to observe another interesting phenomenon: the communal lie or boundary post. We normally term it the former, though it may well be the latter.

The "communal lie" is a large light area on the bottom of the river, that is intermittently crossed by several fish: sometimes singly, sometimes — briefly — by two or even three fish at a time. We have seen the communal lie on several occasions; and in each case the large areas of lighter coloration have clearly been caused not by the action of any one fish, but by the actions of several fish continually crossing and recrossing a fixed point on the riverbed.

With the whole of the river available it is something of a mystery why the fish should, time after time, cross a given point — usually located, we have found, at the extreme downstream ends of their individual beats.

The fish appear on the light patch they have created, linger for a moment or two, and then move on. When more than one fish arrives on the patch at the same time, the individuals show no territorial aggression, but swerve gently off, onto their individual beats.

It has been clear to us that the communal lie is not a feeding or survival lie in the sense that we have discussed them so far: but equally clearly they are points in the water which are shared — if momentarily — by several fish with beats of their own.

The most probable explanation is that the communal lie is a common boundary point that marks the limits to the beat of each fish.

However it comes to be created, the communal lie is an interesting phenomenon. But for practical angling significance, the light patch leaves it standing. The light patch is of profound importance to the angler.

Angler and his companions on the River Test, one of England's famed chalkstreams.➤

The Achilles Heel of the trout lies — if we may be permitted a stiff metaphorical cocktail — in his stomach: in the fact that he must eat to live, and becomes vulnerable the moment he opens his mouth to satisfy himself.

There is, of course, no absolute certainty that because a trout has opened his mouth to take our fly, then he has taken it in mistake for the kind of food he is used to eating (or, for that matter, that he has taken it in mistake for any kind of food at all).

The only certainty about a fish that we bring to the net on a fly, is that it has taken the fly into its mouth *because that is where the fly clearly is when we see it.* Any question of how it came to be there — what motivated the fish to take it into its mouth in the first place — will forever remain hypothesis, unless a fish can be persuaded to talk.

But when that is said, there *are* grounds for assuming that when a fish feeding selectively upon, say, small flies of a particular kind takes a small artificial dressed to imitate such creatures, then that fish has taken the artificial in mistake for the real thing. G.E.M. Skues said he would give up the game if he believed anything else; and a long march of anglers would wind the road behind him, if they did not believe the same. It is the fundamental premise upon which all imitative fly fishing on rivers is based; and it is a premise which all of us accept.*

---

*This is not to say that we believe all trout take feathered confections on hooks, in the belief that they are food. Often we believe, lake trout take lures and streamers out of curiosity and/or aggression. The reader wishing to find a detailed analysis of this subject will find it in Brian Clarke's book *The Pursuit of Stillwater Trout*.

So the challenge for the fly fisherman becomes — how can we exploit this gastronomic chink in the trout's scaly armor: the chink that makes him open his mouth to eat, and that makes him vulnerable the moment he does so?

Far and away the greatest step any angler can take towards capturing the trout is to acquire an understanding of its feeding behavior; and in particular, of the relationship between the behavior of the trout and the kind of insect it wishes to eat.

It is one of the most important things to understand in the whole of fly fishing, that the feeding movements of the trout are not random, and without consequence. Trout move in characteristic ways, when pursuing creatures of different species which are themselves moving in different ways, in and upon the water; and these movements, and the water displacements which result from them when the fish are feeding at or near the surface, can be interpreted to provide golden clues for the fly fisher.

Let us look at them together, now.

THE RISE AS A GUIDE TO THE FLY

The Principle of Interpretation

Elsewhere we have observed that the trout, like all other creatures in the wild, is concerned to save energy.

His desire to do this is not, of course, the product of a thinking process, any more than anything else a trout does is the product of a thinking process. The desire exists simply because that is the way that evolution, and the laws of survival, have chosen to make it.

Given that the trout is concerned not to expend energy uselessly, it is, consequently, a reasonable assumption that in the main, he will not expend more energy in pursuit of an item of food than he will replace by consuming it.

It will, of course, happen from time to time, and on occasion several fish will be seen to do the same — for example, when there is competition for the sudden appearance of a limited amount of a particularly desirable food. But common sense dictates that our premise must by and large be sound, or else the trout would long since have ceased to exist. Over time his ancestors would have grown weaker and weaker; and certainly no creature in the wild needs to ask twice what happens when that deadly descent is begun.

So as a general consequence of our premise, we can reasonably say that if a creature which the trout wants to eat is moving only slowly, then the trout will itself move only slowly, to catch and eat it. And common sense similarly dictates that if a creature which a trout wants to eat is moving at high speed, then the trout itself will simply *have* to move at high speed, if it is to overhaul its prey, and dine.

So the first point that it is necessary to store away in understanding the principle of rise-forms, is that in general trout move slowly when eating slowly moving creatures, and briskly when eating swiftly moving creatures.

In other words, that there is a direct relationship between the speed of the trout, and the locomotive capacities of the insect it wishes to eat.

Now let us look at the water in which the rise-form is revealed, and see what we can deduce from that.

A trout swims — for the sake of simplicity — by thrusting its body from side to side. Each time it thrusts, it displaces the water alongside its flanks. If it swims quickly, it will be thrusting vigorously, and so will displace water with some violence. If it swims slowly, then the more leisurely movements of its body will displace water more gently.

But wait! Does this not mean that there is not only a relationship between the speed of the trout and the speed of the creature it is pursuing, but a relationship, too, between the speed of the trout, and the violence with which the water is displaced?

Yes, indeed.

And does this not now complete the linkage? Do we not have a link between the movement (or absence of movement) on the part of the wee creature at the start of it all, and the water displacement (or rise-form) that we see?

Indeed, dear Watson, it does, and we do. It means that by using our wits and powers of observation, we can look at many kinds of rise-forms and have an excellent idea of the kinds of creatures that might have prompted them, simply by knowing what kinds of creatures move in which kinds of ways, and where.

The discovery of the principles behind movement and rise-forms, is about as close to the Philosopher's Stone that the fly fisherman is likely (or, indeed, would want) to get. With the mental reference points which they provide, let us look now at the rise-forms that can be regularly observed; and let us see what they can tell us about the gastronomic preferences of the fish that cause them.

And let us do something else, as well. Let us see what we can discover from the trout that feeds *below* the surface, regardless of whether or not he can be seen directly, and whether or not he creates a rise-form. Not all fish, even in clearwater, alkaline streams, can be seen all of the time — but that does not mean they are not there. Sometimes it is because they are concealed by reflected light. Sometimes it is because they are concealed by surface ripple. Sometimes it is because they lie deep down in hidden places that are fruitful to them but impenetrable to the human eye.

Indeed, let us look at these most coy among our fishy friends, first. Often — though deliciously unaware of the fact — they reveal where they are, and what they're up to, to the man who is prepared to use his eyes, and to engage his brain behind them.

LOCATING INVISIBLE FISH

Reflections

One of the most common — and the most subtle — of all the ways in which an unseen fish can betray its presence, is by causing a small movement in the otherwise still reflections in the surface film on smooth water.

As we discussed in a previous chapter, there are reflections in the surface of all smooth stretches of river, when the sun is not behind or overhead: reflections of the opposite bank, of trees and buildings; of distant features of the terrain, like hills.

They do not always stay constant in *tone,* because of changes in the intensity of the light; but all reflections will have a constancy of shape and sharpness that is "right" for the reach and conditions at the time. Right, that is, until a fish swims beneath the surface with sufficient violence to shift them.

Then, the reflection of a hitherto straight tree trunk might suddenly acquire a curve, or an S-bend. The outline of a building might blur for a moment or two, at just one point. In an area of dark reflections as we discussed in the matter of seeing fish, small winks of light might suddenly appear. In an area of light, localized patches of dark may briefly be observed.

All these clues — and others besides — are excellent indications of a fish: and a moving (and so possibly

Unseen fish can often reveal their whereabouts by disturbing the surface film as they move to intercept nymphs below it. As these illustrations show, a straight tree trunk might suddenly acquire an S-bend, and the sharp outline of a building or hill might blur at just one point.

feeding) fish at that. It is the man who observes such subtle clues who has a flying start over the man who does not. Simply knowing that a fish is there prompts him to find a position from which the fish itself might become visible. If such a position cannot be attained, a well-placed throw will often bring him a response, nonetheless.

It is, of course, such an occasional, apparently random throw which consistently delivers fish, that gives men reputations for "sixth senses"; or some mysterious communion with the wild. It is nothing of the sort. The "random" throw to the spectator who has missed the clues might merely be the *coup de grace* of the fly fisherman behind the rod.

The Cross-Current Ripple

The water does not have to be silken smooth to reveal the presence of fish which cannot be seen from the bankside. As we mentioned briefly when discussing what the observant angler might expect to see in the water, one of the most common indications of all occurs in rolling, eddying, fast-flowing water.

Eddies and ripples in a river might to a non-fisherman look simply like a confusion of undulations and swirls. But even the tyro fisherman soon comes to see that they are not: that there is a pattern or rhythm to events with, as we observed, always the preponderance of movement occurring in a downstream direction.

While all eddies and ripples are of course different, observation for only a few moments will show what is characteristic of them, on a given piece of water. The telltale clues begin to come, when anything uncharacteristic is thereafter observed.

A common clue occurs when a tress of downstream ripples is momentarily interrupted at some point in its course by a procession of ripples *across the general flow*.

Such a widthways disturbance does not last long — it will be gone in a second or two — but it has almost certainly been caused by a fish whirling to take something below the surface: its sudden lunge has sent an upthrust of water heaving to the top. The "boil" reaches the surface partly dissipated by the force of the current, but holds up long enough to break or disturb the existing rumples.* The result is a series of cross-current ripples.

Such a phenomenon is unmistakable to the man who knows what he is looking for, and all but invisible to the man who does not.

---

*In American usage, irregular creases — *Editor.*

A subtle indication of a trout's presence in broken water, is created by a fish as it turns sharply to intercept an item of food below the surface. The water pushed upwards by the trout's flank reaches the surface, and causes a momentary break in the pattern of ripples created by the downstream flow of the current.

All of the above concerns, of course, an upthrust of water caused by a fish pursuing a nymph in broken water. On slow or smooth water the water will actually appear to bulge when a fish takes a nymph close to the surface.

The Sub-Surface "Rise"

The sub-surface rise is a rise-form that causes more confusion, and more exploration of the Anglo-Saxon vocabulary, than any other.

The problem arises because, in calm water, the disturbance created by a fish taking a nymph, pupa, or shrimp close to the surface, or one of those species of spinners that drifts along just beneath the film, can easily be mistaken for a rise to a surface fly.

The inability to distinguish between the rise to the emerging nymph and the rise to the surface fly proper, is perhaps the single most common cause of failure, when the fish respond to a hatch. Alas, there is no shortcut. The only way the two can be told apart is by practiced observa-

The trickiest rise of all to distinguish . . . and it's easy to see why. The lunge of the trout as it removes a nymph from the underside of the surface film, creates a disturbance that is almost identical to the typical rise to a surface fly. Only careful observation will reveal the truth.

tion. The answer is to look long and hard, before deciding what to offer. And the first step in that process is to watch the fate of any surface flies that you can see drifting over the position of the fish. If these flies are taken, then you have your answer. If they are not taken, or if no surface fly is in evidence, then you've *probably* got your answer and it will be the converse. (Fish, as we shall soon see, are quite capable of taking flies from the surface that are wholly invisible from five yards away.)

The reason that distinction between the surface and sub-surface fly is so important is that a trout preoccupied with sub-surface food is unlikely to rise to surface artificials, no matter how perfectly tied and delicately delivered. The reverse, however, is not the case. The trout that is feeding at the surface is quite often prepared to settle for a nymph, for reasons best understood by itself.

Here the trout has intercepted the ascending nymph a little way below the surface. The whirl it has created is typical of the rise-form created by fish taking nymphs close to the surface. The other common surface disturbance such fish make is a brief welling up or "bulging" of the surface film.

The "Twist"

The interpretation of specific kinds of feeding behavior in fish, is one of the highest levels of sophistication to which the fly fisherman can aspire. It is also one of the most rewarding, in terms of understanding the fish in its environment; and *the* most important, as a means of adding trout to the bag.

The "twist" is a common feeding movement below the water surface, and interpretation of it embodies each of the satisfactions outlined above.

The twist is a semi-corkscrewing action in which the trout — which invariably is lying close to the bottom — rolls on its side for a second or so at a very acute angle to the riverbed, and then resumes its normal, dorsal-up position. It is a movement that can be repeated over and over, revealing the predilection of a fish for shrimps.

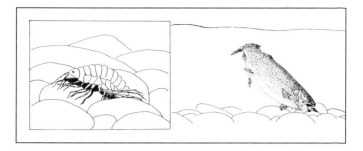

Shrimp clinging to the bottom prompt trout to move in an unusual way to dislodge them.

The shrimp is a furtive creature that lives, when there is no weed about, hard down among the stones on the bottom; clinging onto them hunchbacked, head down, with all his tiny legs. He has a marked lack of enthusiasm for his wider role in the chain of life; and goes out of his way, indeed, to avoid it. When he needs to move, he moves around the sides of stones; and under the arches formed where stones abut; and he clambers down cracks and wrinkles in their surface if traverse them he must, to avoid the attentions of the trout.

So on stony reaches, the trout rarely has the chance to nab a shrimp in mid-water. If he wants a shrimp, he must pick one off the bottom with his mouth.

It is primarily for this reason, we believe, that the trout engages himself in the twist on stony ground. He engages in this behavior because he must; he exhibits such a feeding movement because his mouth is simply the wrong shape for picking a moving, reluctant creature, such as a shrimp, off the surface of a stone.

If the trout wants a shrimp that is crawling along the bottom, *he must roll onto his side, and shovel it off with the flat side of his mouth.*

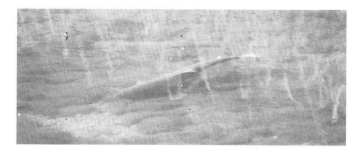

A fascinating aspect of underwater feeding . . . a trout using the flat side of its mouth to shovel up a shrimp clinging determinedly to the bottom. Note the twist motion of the trout.

An occasional secondary purpose of the twist may be to flush shrimps or nymphs from the bottom, so that the trout can take them mid-water. But we believe this purpose to *be* secondary because only infrequently is a fish seen to make the characteristic dart and snap at mid-water food, once the body twist has been completed. The twist, almost always, is a self-contained action.

The "Tailing" Trout

"Tailing" is a feeding activity which bridges the gap — literally and metaphorically — between fish feeding below the surface, and those *at* the surface; an activity which often sees the tail of the fish waving in the air while it is busy removing goodies from weedbeds and the bottom, in very shallow water. It is a rise-form that — even for the sophisticated fisherman — can pose problems of distinction, unless it is observed from close quarters.

The tailing fish is most often feeding upon shrimps, nymphs, aquatic snails and caddis. As its head goes down its tail comes up and breaks the surface film, either continuously or spasmodically.

The tailing trout — in shallow water — can create problems of interpretation unless observed at close quarters. The disturbance his tail can leave in the surface film can often appear very like a rise to a spent surface fly, when seen from some distance away.

When the tail is almost continuously above the surface film — by half an inch, an inch or more — the effect is very much like that caused by a single stem of reed which breaks the surface: a fine V of water runs downstream for a short distance before the current thins it out, and causes the disturbance to disappear. It is an easy matter, because of this, to walk by a tailing fish that feeds in shallow margins, or in reaches abounding with reeds. When the tail breaks the surface only spasmodically, the effect is very much like a rise to the spent fly or "spinner" that is trapped in the surface film.

The "Head-and-Tail" Rise

The "head-and-tail" rise is the nearest thing to a surface rise that the trout actually makes without, as it were, going all the way. Few sights set the fly fisherman's adrenalin flowing more swiftly.

The head-and-tail rise always seems to happen in breathless slow motion, frame by cinematic frame: first the top of the head appears; then the shoulders, back and dorsal fin; and finally that big, broad tail.

It seems to be a characteristic of the rise that it flatters the size of the fish which makes it. A head-and-tailing trout always seems to be some kind of sinuous and utterly monstrous submarine; yet when it comes out, it looks extraordinarily like a trout, and extraordinarily like an ordinary trout, at that.

Perhaps the most languid, classical rise-form of all, the head-and-tail rise, a pattern typical of the trout intercepting small duns, and some spinners and nymphs trapped by the surface film. Here the tail of the fish waves its contemptuous goodbye.

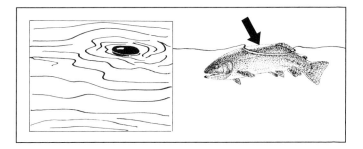

The Head-and-Tail Rise

The head-and-tail rise is rarely seen in fast-flowing, broken water or rapids. It is a phenomenon of the smoother reaches; and it is usually to nymphs or spinners that have become trapped below the surface film; and to midge pupae similarly immobilized.

SURFACE RISE-FORMS

The "Sip" or "Kiss" Rise

In our view, though we have chosen to deal with it in its strict position in the sequence of events, the "sip" or "kiss" rise is the most interesting of all the rise-forms that the fly fisherman sees. It is also the rise that enables us to demonstrate most comprehensively how careful observation and a little thought can be combined to produce an insight into the world of the fish, and the techniques that might be employed to deceive him. We will examine the rise in detail.

The sip or kiss rise embodies two very distinct characteristics. The first is the distinct, audible kissing noise we hear; the second is a small, pinpoint, almost imperceptible disturbance of the surface film — little more than an

No need to hurry . . . A quiet rise — usually accompanied by a brief sipping or kissing noise — is almost always made to flies trapped in or immediately under the surface film, that the fish knows from experience cannot get away.

ebbing full stop that is swiftly contorted and then dispersed by the moving current.

In attempting to fathom the secret of the kiss, the first question that needs to be answered is, "Why should a fish taking in food make a kissing noise?" Or put another way, "What must a fish making such a noise be doing?"

And what does common sense suggest the answer must be? It suggests that a fish making a kissing noise is *not only* sucking in flies. To make that audible sip, it *must* be taking in a little water *and air as well* (try sipping hot soup off a spoon, and see what we mean).

And what does this reveal? It reveals that of all the depths at which fish can feed, the one we are interested in is feeding right at the surface film, *because that is where the air is located.*

The second important point that can be deduced is that the trout we are watching is swimming very slowly, if, indeed, it is swimming at all (and the trout, like the sea gull on a breeze, does not have to work to move: he can simply adjust his fins, and float up on the current).

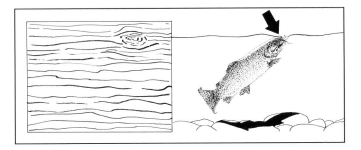

The kiss rise is one of the most fascinating of all rise forms. It has two characteristics: (a) an audible sipping noise created by the brief but powerful suck that the trout uses to bring the fly (and with it some air) down to its position in the water; and (b) the tiniest dimpling disturbance that it creates in the surface film.

How can we deduce that the fish is not swimming at any kind of speed? Because we know the fish is right at the surface (where the air is) and yet is making only the tiny surface disturbance that we can see: that punctilious, ebbing full stop. *And would not a fish traveling quickly right at the surface create a commotion, because of the water he would displace?*

Indeed he would. (It is an aside — but one worth making here. The very gentleness of the sip rise is often indicative of a large trout that has learned to feed on surface food, while expending the minimum amount of energy. Very large trout rarely make a commotion when feeding.)

There is a third point that can reasonably be deduced from this rise. It is that the fish is absolutely certain that the creature it is after is motionless in the surface film, and cannot get away.

How? Because, attentive dear Watson, of the utterly confident, leisurely and precise way that he sucks in the fly. If the fly had any serious chance of escape — if it had wings up and was capable of making off — instinct and experience would have told an animal that survives by ensuring an adequate return on its output of energy, to hurry things along. Just because the trout has *not* hurried things along, it is a sound assumption it knows it has no need: we have already established that, nine times out of ten, a creature in the wild only moves briskly when it absolutely has to.

And so we're almost there. There is only one question left that the fly fisherman must ask before putting up an appropriate artificial, and casting it with a high degree of confidence. It is: what flies can we expect to find in or on the surface film (where the air is) that cannot get away (because the fish shows no urgency when intercepting them)? And the answer to that, of course, is only flies that are dead or dying, and that are trapped *by* the surface film.

Many flies, of course, find a watery grave; but those which most commonly promote the "sipping" rise are the "spent" spinners that have collapsed onto the water to die, after laying their eggs. Their legs collapse or break through the film, their bodies break into it, and their wings adhere, cruciform, to its treacherous cloy.

After the spent fly, perhaps the most common creature to die at the surface is the hatching nymph.

Not all aquatic flies manage to extricate themselves cleanly from the nymphal shuck. A great many fail to pull their bodies clear; or else they get a wing caught in the nymphal sleeve, or one or more wings stuck, like the spent fly, to the surface. Still others do not give themselves the opportunity to die from natural causes. In their desperate struggles to pull themselves free they send out a thousand tiny, ebbing rings — and so attract attention to themselves. And if there is one thing that the trout seems unable to resist, it is the sight of a struggling fly that cannot get away.

(In heavy hatches of fly, indeed, the trout can be observed to occupy himself not with the plain-sailing dun, but with the dun that flutters about before it becomes airborne. These unfortunates semaphore their presence to the fish, and self-select themselves for eating.)

Yet another kind of insect that gets caught in the surface film, as opposed to the creature which stands *on* the surface film, is the terrestrial fly, beetle or grub which falls onto the water. Such animals are wholly unequipped for the aquatic life; and as they struggle, so they penetrate deeper into the film, and at the same time become weaker and weaker — much, appalling thought that it is, like the man who falls into a marsh.

The effect is very much the same; and the end is usually just as assured.

The "Slash"

No rise-form to surface food could be in sharper contrast to the pinpoint delicacy of the kiss rise, than the rise we have termed the "slash". Like the kiss rise, however, it can be interpreted with a little thought.

The slash rise is exactly what the term suggests — a powerful, large-scale disturbance of the surface, in which either spray is hurled high into the air, or there is a powerful, lateral surfing of water.

For exactly the reasons that the delicate and pinpoint kiss was made by a slow-moving fish at the surface, so the slash is created by a fast-moving fish at the surface (how else could the water be broken with such violence?).

If a fish is moving quickly at the surface it is not doing so in order to exhaust itself. There are, no doubt, exceptions. There are village idiots among fish, just as there

A high-speed slash, as a big trout hurls itself after a departing sedge. No creature in the wild expends more energy than it has to, and a violent rise-form like this is almost always to a large insect that the trout knows could easily escape.

are village idiots among men. But in the main, as we have discussed, fish move just as fast as they have to, and no faster. And if a trout is consistently moving at high speed at the surface (and even more certainly, if several fish are moving at high speed at the surface) it is because it is having to do so in order to catch a prey which is either itself moving at high speed, or which the fish knows from either experience or instinct, is *capable* of moving at high speed, and escaping.

The most common fly that causes the trout to move briskly upon it is the sedge or caddis.

Many species of caddis are large, as flies go, and are therefore tempting on this ground alone. But some species of caddis set up an enormous commotion on the water when they hatch; or when they scutter across the surface, to lay their eggs.

The scuttering V-wake of the latter, and the flutterings that the former creates, awake the predatory instincts of nearby fish; and the capacity — whether latent or apparent — for high-speed movement on the part of the fly results in a high-speed response on the part of the trout.

Because the sedges are in the main nocturnal creatures — they tend to hatch in the evenings, and lay their eggs in the evenings — then the slashing rise is most commonly an evening phenomenon. If there is a slashing rise during the day, then the angler who knows the nighttime predilections of most of the sedges will turn his mind to other beasts. And the candidate highest on the list will be a large terrestrial insect that has deposited itself upon the surface or, of course, during its relatively short season, the Mayfly (Green Drake).

The Waggle

The "waggle" — for want of a more elegant though less descriptive term — is not a common rise-form. It is, however, important to draw attention to it, so that it can be distinguished from the head-and-tail rise.

The waggle is a rise-form in which the shoulders, dorsal fin and tail of the fish are visible in the surface film, almost simultaneously. It is a phenomenon of smooth water of uniform flow; and denotes a fish feeding — often besottedly — on small Ephemeropteran duns and spinners drifting down in flotillas upon the current.

It is a languid rise: a rise clearly made by a fish that has had a good sighting of its prey, and that has simply drifted up into the surface from its position just below. It is a rise made by a fish that has almost lain in wait for the fly to drift into its mouth. There is the merest trace of forward propulsion as the fish, mouth closing and turning down from the horizontal, shrugs his way below the film again.

The last part of the trout's anatomy to disappear is its tail. Someone, a long time ago, described the languid

Angler on the Malleo River, Argentina.

shrug as "a satisfied wag of the tail". It is an apt and accurate description, for more than one reason. The trout has acquired his natural fly, and not taken our artificial. The waggling trout rarely gets caught on the artificial fly, in our experience.

The Plain Rise

The "plain" rise is the straightforward removal of a dun or other creature, from the surface of the water.

It is a plain, unromantic, unexotic rise that does not have outstanding characteristics: no sips or kisses, no slashes at the surface, no languid rolls. It is a rise for all seasons — an Ombudsrise — and it can occur almost anywhere. The trout simply sees the fly — usually a dun — swims up to it, opens its mouth and takes it in, before rolling away.

The plain rise occurs in both swift water and slow, and the manifestations of it will change with the character of the water.

(All rises, of course, are to some extent dependent upon the character and speed of the water and, indeed, upon the amount of fly available, and the depth at which the fish is lying. It is interesting to note that these factors can lead to different kinds of specific rise-form even when only one kind of fly is involved — the dead or dying fly trapped in the surface film. On slow reaches, close to the bank, the typical rise to such creatures in a heavy "fall" would be the sip rise: the sip tends to be more characteristic of trout lying close to the bank. In midstream, where the water is somewhat faster, the fish taking such creatures in a heavy fall will probably rise with a head-and-tail motion, or perhaps with a waggle. If the fall is sparse, however, then a plain rise will ensue: the fish seeking food that is only sparsely available will lie deeper to give himself a wider field of view. And his trajectory and speed in coming up from the depths and returning to them creates a more vigorous disturbance than that made by his longitudinal friend mentioned above. The head-and-tail, the sip and the waggle are all created by fish lying close to the surface where the fish has a small field of view. They are, therefore, suggestive of fish with plenty of flies passing over them — and so all are rises seen in heavy hatches or falls.)

In slow water, there will be a positive, circular, ebbing of rings, sometimes accompanied by an audible smacking noise. In fast, rippled water there will be a peremptory interruption of the flow, combined with a brief cross-ripple similar to that described for a nymphing fish in fast water — though more pronounced. In water that is swift and unbroken the rise will show immediately as a ring, but will then be swept away to nothingness, in a yard or two.

In other words, the basic movement of the fish is always consistent, and it is only the water that changes. In the creation of many of the more specialized rise-forms it is the movement of the fish that alters.

There is one last point that we would make, that is important to the observation of rise-forms in general, and surface rise-forms in particular. There is one characteristic clue that the surface-feeding fish leaves behind that the sub-surface feeder does not. It is a clue that can help to separate the two, when the rise itself goes unobserved.

It is: bubbles.

When a trout takes a fly from the surface, it cannot help but take in some air as well. When a trout does take in air, it gets rid of it as rapidly as it possibly can, by opening its gills. And because the trout is well below the water's surface when the gills are opened, the air rises to the surface as a bubble or bubbles.

In calm water, therefore, if the light is awkward and it is difficult to see whether the rise has been through the surface film or just below it, look for the telltale bubbles.

The Myth of the Kidney-Shaped Whirl

The greatest liberator of the human mind in fly fishing this century was G.E.M. Skues, whom we have previously mentioned. That is our view. From the time he first appeared in print in a letter to *The Field* in the 1890s, to his death in the late 1940s, Skues brought more insight, perception and common sense to fly-fishing literature than any other angler of whom we know or have heard.

But understandably, in the course of such a long and communicative life, there are some points on which Skues was mistaken — or mistaken, at least, in our view. We will touch upon one of these points now, because it has passed into the folklore of fly fishing: and in particular, into the folklore of English fly fishing.

That point is the cause of what Skues described as the "kidney-shaped whirl", a name he gave to the rise-form he associated with the Blue-Winged Olive so beloved of the chalkstream angler.

Since Skues described this rise-form and its "characteristic" kidney-shaped double whirl, two generations of anglers to date — as no doubt will several to come — have scanned the water for it, when the Blue-Winged Olive has been expected. The kidney-shaped whirl has become a "classical" rise-form, like the sip or the slash.

What the eye has not seen, the mind has imposed; and the supposed observation of it, has led to the hasty delivery of the Blue-Winged Olive in its artificial form.

There is no such rise-form as the kidney-shaped whirl. More precisely, a disturbance not unlike a kidney shape may occasionally be made by a feeding fish but such a disturbance *is characteristic of nothing,* ninety-nine times out of a hundred. The one-hundredth time, a kidney-type shape may appear on the water surface, but that will have been created by a fish that has risen to one fly, turning away at the last moment to take another. The so-called kidney-shaped displacement of water occurs no more frequently as a response to a particular insect, than as any other contortion of the water surface that the observer might dignify with a name.

When a fish moves to intercept a fly, it displaces water. And it is true that there is a direct relationship between the speed of the fish, and the violence with which the water is disturbed. But the disturbance itself can and does take on almost *any* shape, give or take a broad circular movement that is influenced by the current, once the action is over.

There is no species of insect that would require a fish to move in a way that would consistently result in a kidney-shaped whirl, any more than there is, say, a species of sedge that would result in the eruption of the slashing rise taking on, say, a crown shape, or a steeple shape, or a ship shape.

However, the kidney-shaped whirl is now imprinted upon the mind of the fly fisher. It is a handy picture that he can see in his mind's eye and often *expects to see* on the water. The deception is a self-deception, very close indeed to the kind of process through which the trout apparently goes when he expects to see a fly, and rises to something with a nasty sharp hook inside it.

Happily, the results are less severe. If they were not, indeed, there would be very few fly fishers left — and no fishers to the rise to the Blue-Winged Olive at all.

OVERLEAF: *Playing a rainbow on the Madison River, Montana.*

PART TWO

VISION: TROUT AND MAN

HOW THE TROUT SEES

In the first part of this book we have considered the trout and his environment from the dry seclusion of our position on the bankside. To the layman standing on the edge of a clear stream or lake, wherein every weed and stone is clearly visible, there might seem no good reason why one should go further: why the trout looking upwards should not have a similar view to the one that we have looking downwards — though, of course, in reverse.

The fact is, however, that there are several good reasons why the trout does not, and cannot, see things as we see them; and an excursion below the surface will not only give the observer new insights into trout behavior, but a better understanding of the angling techniques that he might employ.

In view of its profound importance to the angler, it is surprising to us that the great mass of angling literature has ignored the question of fish vision, and the factors which influence it.

The first author to touch upon the subject, briefly, was Alfred Ronalds in *The Fly-Fisher's Entomology*, published in the middle of the nineteenth century. Since then only a handful of writers have looked at fish vision in any detail. The most notable of these have been Dr. Francis Ward in *Animal Life Under Water* (1919) — a book that was far ahead of its time; J.W. Dunne in *Sunshine and the Dry Fly* (1924) — an interesting and unusual work; Col. E.W. Harding in *The Fly-Fisher and the Trout's Point of View* (1931) — much the most thorough study of the subject published up to that point; and E.R. Hewitt in *A Trout and Salmon Fisherman for Seventy-five Years* (1948). More recently a beautiful book published in the United States by Vincent Marinaro — *In the Ring of the Rise* — has discussed aspects of the subject; and *Through the Fish's Eye* by Mark Sosin and John Clark, also published in the United States, likewise should be mentioned.

But when one has said that, one has said most of it. It is also important to note that even those books that have discussed the subject — including some of those mentioned above — have incorporated either basic misunderstandings that have led their authors to some incorrect conclusions, or else have been based upon a level of scientific knowledge which has since been superseded again leading their authors to some incorrect conclusions (or, at least, to conclusions which appear to be incorrect today: one thing no one can yet say is how the brain of a fish *interprets* the messages transmitted from the eyes).

Light, the "Window" and the "Mirror"

Any discussion of what the trout can see — and of the relevance of this to angling technique — can only sensibly begin with an examination of the means by which the trout sees anything.

Such a discussion will focus on *light* (without which nothing could be seen by anything); and the capacities of the fish's eye itself. The former will take us into the world

These illustrations demonstrate clearly the effects of the refraction or bending of light. The mark on the stick is half way down its length, and the stick itself is touching the bottom. In the illustration on the left, refraction makes the stick appear to be shorter than it actually is. Because therefore we know that the end of the stick is further away than it seems, we know that the river or lake bed is also further away: in other words, the water is deeper than appearances might suggest.

In the illustration on the right, the bending of light is made quite visible. The stick, of course, is straight, but it appears to bend sharply where it cuts through the surface. One of the most practical effects of refraction for the angler — when he is trying to judge the exact position of a trout in the water — is made clear by the illustration on the next page.

of the "window" and the "mirror"; and the latter, given today's knowledge of the structure and physics of the eye, will give us an appreciation of what the trout is capable of seeing in that world.

Light is the medium by which anything is seen; and in the natural world of the outdoors, all light originates from

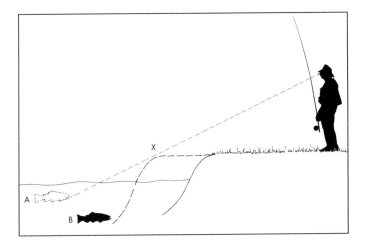

The illustration shows, in a figurative way, what refraction can mean to the angler. The angler sees his trout at position A — but the actual position of the trout is at B. In other words, fish appear to be lying less deep in the water than they really are. Note also that if the bank went out to the point marked "X", the angler would still see the fish, even though a straight line drawn between his eyes and the true position of the trout would now be cut off by the bank. Thus, refraction enables the angler to see around corners. Alas, it also enables the trout to do the same!

the sun. It comes to us as a continuous wave, but for our purposes here is best described as an infinite number of individual "rays".

It is these rays which carry the images of our surroundings into our eyes, and enable objects to be seen.

These rays of light from the sun travel in a straight line through the air (which is not a dense medium) until they reach the water (which is).

Then, at the point at which these rays enter the water, they bend. Anyone who has thrust a stick into the water will have seen it foreshorten or bend. This is the refraction of light, made visible.

However, not all rays of light are capable of entering the water to the same extent. The lowest rays to carry a useful image to any given point below the surface (for example, the eye of a trout) coincide with the surface at an angle of about 10 degrees to the horizontal.*

The lowest rays bend where they enter the water at an angle of about 48.5 degrees to the vertical. Rays entering the water *above* 10 degrees to the horizontal, bend less and less until they reach a single ray that falls into the water from directly overhead, and that does not bend at all. The illustration on the next page makes this clear.

This illustration also shows how, in a cross section of the world of the trout, the only useful light that reaches the eye of the trout (or any other point below the surface) is contained within an *external* arc of some 160 degrees (180 degrees less the 10 degrees or so at either side that carry little useful light into the water); and anything outside the water that the trout sees clearly, must be contained within this arc.

It is this field of view where it enters the water, that is known as the trout's window. It is an appropriate choice of word: a "window" to the outside world.

The image that the trout receives through this window is not a uniform one. It is obvious that if an external arc of approximately 160 degrees is compressed by refraction

---

*Although rays below 10 degrees *do* enter the water surface we are, in light of our experiments discussed on page 121, regarding 10 degrees as the effective cut-off point. So little light penetrates the water from below this level, that the images conveyed become ever darker and more meaningless.

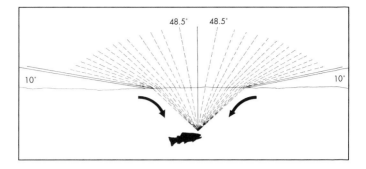

The external field of view of the trout (his window), showing how some 160 degrees of useful view outside the water, is funneled down by refraction into 97 degrees below water. The illustration is, of course, a cross section: the trout sees all around it at the surface, and its window is circular. This illustration also gives a figurative impression of how the greatest crowding of rays of light occurs at the outside edge of the window, at the point at which they enter the water. It is this crowding and bending of rays that results in most of the images the fish receives around its window, being distorted.

into an arc of approximately 97 degrees (the illustration above again) there must be a high degree of distortion. The greatest degree of distortion — which results in objects appearing shorter and consequently wider than they really are — occurs at the outside edge of the window, where the light rays are most bent and most compressed.

The distortion gets less and less until directly overhead (where, remember, the light does not bend) things are seen in true outline against the sky.

The illustration on the opposite page shows another interesting point concerning the trout's view of the world above water. It is that because his "ground level" is light coming in at an angle of 48.5 degrees to the vertical, all the images that this light carries will be positioned at that angle above him. The effect is as though he were looking

How the trout sees the world above the water. First, because only light that penetrates the surface from about 10 degrees or above carries useful images to him, any part of an external object that lies below this 10 degrees is cut off at the 10-degree line, for all practical purposes.

Secondly, because the lowest rays of light bend where they enter the water and reach his eye at an angle of 48.5 degrees from the vertical, the trout sees everything from an angle of 48.5 degrees or less. He simply has no way of knowing that the angle outside the water is a mere 10 degrees. As a result, "ground level" to the trout is a permanent steep hill. This gives him the impression that most of what he can see outside is displaced to a point far above his head.

Note two other points: (a) because light coming to the trout from immediately overhead does not bend, the bird is neither displaced nor distorted; (b) outside that line going up from his eye at 48.5 degrees, the trout sees nothing of the outside world. Everything around his window is a mirror image of the weeds and bottom around him.

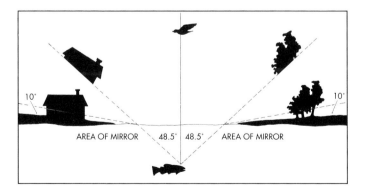

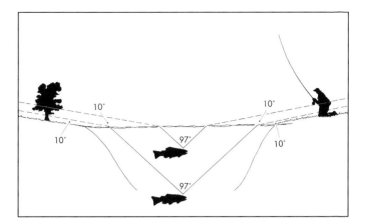

The apex of the trout's cone of vision is fixed by the laws of refraction at 97 degrees, and so the area of the window will get smaller as the fish nears the surface, and greater as the fish moves away.

up a permanently steep hill with all the objects in the world outside displaced to a point far over his head.

Before moving on to the mirror, there is one last point that we would make. It is that because the angles of the cone of vision are fixed by the laws of refraction, they are constant. For the trout, the effect is that his window moves with him wherever he goes; and gets smaller in area as he nears the surface, and greater in area as he moves away from it (as illustrated above).

In theory, because some light enters the window from every point of the compass and from every level down to the horizontal, the trout's field of view *will be constant regardless of the depth to which he swims. In practice, however, as we state elsewhere, very little light indeed enters the water from below an angle of 10 degrees to the horizontal. As a consequence, the lower trout in the illustration really can see more than his friend above.*

And now the mirror. Because it is only through his window that he can see into the outside world, the trout is by definition surrounded by a large area of water surface through which he cannot see. When the water is calm and unbroken, this area reflects the world on the underside of the surface film; and it is this reflective area that has been dubbed — again appropriately — the mirror.

It should not be imagined that the mirror recedes into the distance like the ceiling of some vast, unsteady room. It does not. To the trout lying close to it, the mirror appears to slope sharply down around him like the roof of a bell tent with its top sliced off (which approximates his window). In front of him, the appearance is very like a cinema screen sloping down sharply to a horizon in the near middle-distance.

Because this optical effect places much of the mirror comfortably in front of the trout (and in the area which he can address with both eyes simultaneously) it seems likely that the mirror has more importance in his feeding behavior than might at first be supposed.

We would add just two important points on the mirror and the window, here. The first is that everything that we have discussed so far concerns the effects of optical laws. The figures that we have quoted can therefore be taken as fact. And because we have been discussing the effects of optical laws, the passages above have nothing at all to do with the properties of the eye of the trout. The trout is wholly subject to the phenomena discussed above, regardless of the properties of his eye.

The second point we would add is one of great importance to the angler. It is that the window and the mirror are separated by a fine circle of iridescent colors — a spectrum — that is known as Snell's Circle. In first observing this circle Mr. Snell performed us all a great service, the full significance of which, so far as we can see, has been missed by everyone who has written on the fish's window and mirror, to date. This significance is discussed in some detail, later in this chapter.

The Eye of the Trout

There are a number of superficial similarities between the human eye, and the eye of the trout. Each, for example, has a cornea, an iris and a lens; and each has a retina carrying light-sensitive cells ("rods" and "cones") that detect the image that is formed upon them.

But that does not mean that the two eyes work in a similar way. Indeed, it would be surprising, to say the least, if eyes that had evolved for use in utterly different media had ended up as much the same kinds of device.

The most significant differences of relevance to the angler lie in the shapes of the respective lenses, and in the means of focusing.

The reason why the two lenses and the focusing mechanisms have evolved so differently, can be readily understood from our discussion of refraction: from the fact that light travels in a straight line through one medium, and bends or refracts when it enters another medium of greater or lesser density.

For a man to see, light must pass from the rare medium of air into the dense fluid of the eye. In so doing, in obedience to the laws of refraction, it bends. The point of entry into the human eye is the curved cornea; and so it is here that considerable initial focusing, through refraction, occurs. The lens in the human eye simply acts as a fine-focusing device, on an image that has already begun to be formed.

In the case of the trout, things are very different. The light reaching him enters the fluid of his eye from another

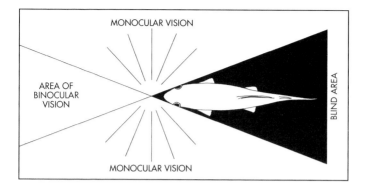

The trout's range of vision. Because his wide-angle eyes are set into the sides of his head, there is only one small area in front of him where the fields of view that they encompass, overlap. It is this area of binocular vision that enables him to judge distance. On either side of his head, he can see only with the one eye that is facing in each direction. His monocular vision is enough to alert him to movement, but he cannot tell how far away that movement is unless he turns full-face on, to look. He cannot see into the area behind him, because it is outside the range of either eye.

fluid all around it — the water. As a consequence, no significant refraction occurs at the point of contact, and so the cornea plays no real part in focusing an image. It is the *lens* of the fish that provides the sole means of focusing. It is to meet this burden that the lens of the trout has evolved into a very powerful mechanism indeed, compared with the lens of man. Whereas the lens in the human eye is fairly flat, the lens in the trout's eye has evolved into a sphere.

Several points of great importance to the angler flow from this.

Because the lens of the fish is a sphere set into the side of its head, the trout has a field of view of some 180 degrees with each eye. That much was hitherto documented and well known.

What is not at all well known is that from a short distance out from its eye the trout can focus simultaneously on a whole range of objects on any given plane, right across this immense field of vision.

This marvelous facility is made possible by the way the light-sensitive cells — the rods and the cones — are grouped on the retina. In man, who only needs a narrow arc of concentrated focus because he can move his head from side to side to cover as wide an area as he wishes, the cones (which are responsible for the detection of color and detail) are concentrated in a small area at the back of the retina — the fovea. In the case of the trout, which likewise needs a wide field of focus as a survival mechanism but which *cannot* move his head with such ease, the cones are distributed much more widely across his retina, as a compensating device. (The rods, which are responsible for vision in dim light and cannot detect either color or detail, are much more evenly distributed over the retina in both man and fish.)

The ability of the trout to look and focus — literally — out of both corners of each eye simultaneously is something that, to the best of our knowledge, has not been documented before in fly-fishing literature; and it has immense significance to the angler. It means that the fish can see — and in an active meaning of the term — in almost every direction at once. Even though, for example, he is looking intently at a fly advancing towards him on the current, he can see you advancing on his flank, with considerable ease. To say the least, this poses a fascinating picture of the kind of thing that must go on in the brain of the trout as he "juggles" with events being transmitted to him, and allocates them priorities of interest.

The trout's ability to see and focus through 180 degrees meets another need that any predator has — *binocular* vision. It is binocular vision that enables both the trout, and us, to judge *distance*.

The trout obtains binocular vision in the area most important to him — directly in front, where his mouth is — from the fact that his two 180 degree eyes are positioned slightly towards the front of his head, where the frontal limits of the arc of vision can overlap. The penalty that the trout pays for his binocular vision in front is that he has a corresponding blind area behind. The illustration on page 89 makes clear how binocular vision is achieved in the trout.

Before moving on to the other specific aspects of trout vision, there is one more point that we wish to make about the trout's eye itself. It concerns the use that this remarkable mechanism can make of the available light.

Using the terminology that is employed to define the light-gathering capacities of photographic lenses, the human eye has been shown to have an effective aperture of approximately f2.0. By contrast, the effective aperture of the trout's eye has been shown to be approximately f1.2. This means (because the scale is inversely proportional, and the smaller the f number the greater the amount of light the lens admits) that if the eye of the trout were the same size as the eye of man, it would admit *three times* the amount of light. Even at the size that it is, it seems likely that the vision of the trout in poor light will be better than that of the angler pursuing him.

(It is a point of interest that the mathematics of fishes' eyes was worked out well over one hundred years ago by the British physicist James Clerk Maxwell, whose curiosity, oddly enough, was stimulated not by the trout, alas, but by the eye of his breakfast kipper!)

Focusing and Its Relevance

It will be apparent from what we have already said that the trout's eye is a most remarkable device; one that has evolved to give him, among other capacities, a wide field of vision, binocular vision, almost all-round focusing and the rest. There is an aspect of this latter quality — his focusing — that is so interesting that we want to deal with it separately.

It concerns the fish's *depth* of focus, and the point at which his eye becomes focused for "infinity".

If the reader feels that such considerations are over technical and can have little practical significance, we would ask him to bear with us for a moment. The fact is that each of these considerations is of fundamental importance in the business of stalking a trout, and presenting it with a fly.

The principles of depth of focus or "depth of field" can best be established by referring again to the focusing mechanism of a modern camera with, say, its lens fully open (the trout cannot adjust its aperture like a camera lens, and so must always use its eye "fully open").

With a camera, there is a point at which the device can be focused (usually around 30 feet distant) beyond which *everything* comes into focus: the depth of field reaches to "infinity".

As the lens is focused nearer and nearer, the depth of field that is in focus gets less and less until, when the lens is focused at the nearest point to which it *can* be focused (usually about 18 inches) the depth of field is little more than paper-thick. On either side of that narrow plane, everything is out of focus.

Consider, now, the trout. All the observations that we have made so far about what he can see, and that other writers have tended to concentrate upon, have been based upon the assumption that the fish is focused for infinity. That is clearly, for example, the only way he is going to see distant objects through his window.

But of course, the trout is *not* always focused for infinity, any more than we are. And would it not be useful to know what is and is not in focus, when he is looking at objects at different distances? Indeed it would. Such information, for example, would tell us whether we are in focus at all, or so out of focus as to be invisible for all practical purposes *whether or not we are in his window.* Such information, likewise, would give us an insight into why one trout will move only an inch or two to intercept a fly drifting towards it, when another will move several feet: and so on.

We began with observation in the field.

We had already come to the conclusion that the trout was capable of focusing to within an inch, or a little more, of the end of his nose. We had studied hundreds of fish, on many different rivers, in many different circumstances, dropping downstream with their eyes that close to flies on the surface, and had no doubts about the internal limit of focusing, at all.

We had likewise come to the conclusion that fish feeding very close to the water's surface, had a very small depth of focus. So that, for example, in a heavy hatch of fly, the trout will take up a holding station within two or three inches of the water's surface.

Such a fish will not move more than four or five inches to either side to take a fly. We concluded that the *absence* of such tiny lateral movements reflected the fact not so much that the fish was disinclined to shift, but that flies beyond this distance were invisible to him: that they were outside of his depth of field, when he was focusing on subjects so close to him.

We also noted that trout lying quite well down — say between 18 inches and three feet — would commonly move two, three, four and even five feet to intercept a fly or nymph. This type of behavior seemed to indicate that when a trout was focusing at two feet or more his depth of field was enormously increased and, indeed, in all probability extended to even beyond infinity. When this observation is taken with the fish last mentioned above, it can be suggested that the point where the depth of field extends to infinity, occurred somewhere between three inches and two feet.

But we wanted, if we could get it, something more concrete than a series of simple deductions and we took the problem to Professor W.R.A. Muntz, of the Department of Biology at Stirling University. Professor Muntz has made a professional study of fish and fish behavior and is, specifically, one of the world's leading authorities on fish vision.

Professor Muntz constructed for us the following table based upon his work at the university and upon the following assumptions.

It is assumed that the trout's eye has a diameter of half an inch, and that it is accurately focused to the various distances shown in the top line of the table. It is also assumed that the fish will fail to recognize objects accurately when they are so out of focus that any specific point on them is blurred into a circle half of a degree across on the retina. Effectively, therefore, we have assumed that accurate vision is lost when something like the cross-sectional tip of a rod is so blurred as to appear the width of a U.S. quarter seen from about three paces away. It is a point of interest that calculations done for various other degrees of out-of-focus showed surprisingly little effect on the results.

THE TROUT'S DEPTH OF ACCURATE VISION									
Distance at which eye is focused									
1	2	3	4	6	10	15	20	23	25
Furthest distance at which accurate vision is possible									
1.033	2.16	3.39	4.76	7.97	17.15	39.37	104.17	312.5	X

(All measurements in inches; X = infinity)

This table bears out our field observations to an almost startling degree; it would indeed seem that the point from which the trout can "see to infinity" occurs very close indeed to its eye, and in all probability occurs at something less than two feet.

One important point arising from this, and demonstrated by the table, concerns the question of stalking trout. Such practical observations as we have made, and the table above, suggest that where an angler finds a trout feeding within a very few inches of the surface, then he can approach that fish very much nearer than he could a trout feeding a foot or two deeper: he is likely to be out of focus to the fish feeding very high in the water, and is likely to remain undetected whether or not he falls within its window.

He should likewise note, however, that we are here discussing only *form*. There is nothing at all to say that because a fish cannot see an approaching angler's form very clearly, that it will not be able to detect his movement if he does not take care. And if the fish *is* alerted by a sudden, out-of-focus movement all he has to do is to alter focus, for the angler to come sharply into view.

Color Vision

Do freshwater fish, including trout, have color vision? More particularly, perhaps, do they have the ability to distinguish between *different* colors? The answer, unequivocally, is yes.

There are many reasons for this certainty, including recent evaluation of the properties of the fish's eye by the use of electrodes to tap messages sent along the nerves from the eye to the brain. For the layman, however, all of that may be rather too chilling. The most simple and readily acceptable reason for believing that fish can see color stems from the behavioral studies carried out on them, in laboratories.

Quite simply, in tests carried out in many laboratories in Britain, the United States, Germany and elsewhere, by scientists including Professor Muntz, fish have been *trained to respond* to different colors. Time and again, in demand-feeding experiments, they have shown that they can not only unerringly distinguish between different colors, but between different shades of the same color. In such experiments, the fish get fed if they respond correctly to one color, and they do not get fed if they respond to a different color. Even the *sensitivity* of color vision has been successfully tested, using this simple and well-tried formula: the fish are shown a "food" color over and over but ever more weakly, until they simply fail to react to it.

It is interesting to note that, even given their small brains, the fish used in these experiments showed themselves to be quick learners. (Many of the fish Professor Muntz used in his experiments learned to distinguish between two colors in less than five trials: i.e. they made only one or two errors altogether!) It seems likely that the unerring selection of the correct colors by fish once trained, is not unconnected with the fact that almost half their brain is deployed in the use and control of the visual faculties.

What colors do fish see best? In freshwater, experiments have shown that the color that fish see most easily is red. The next most visible colors are orange and yellow, in that order. The colors that fish see least easily are green and blue. These results have been obtained in conditions of normal light; they do not take account of the changes of color that occur in very deep water.

Scientific studies have also shown that fish can see contrasting patterns or shades (particularly stripes, and to a lesser extent spots) with exceptional clarity. This may account to some extent for the effectiveness of the most popular wet flies on stillwaters — flies that incorporate red or orange in the body or tag, and that employ speckled feathers like teal and mallard, for the wing.

Many examples of these types of patterns come readily to mind — Peter Ross, Mallard and Claret, Parmachene Belle, Dunkeld, Teal and Silver, and many more besides.* We would like to draw attention, however, to the precise and careful wording that we have employed here. The fact that certain colors or contrasts of colors are more conspicuous to fish, does not necessarily mean that fish are more attracted to them.

Night Vision

Most writers seem to agree that trout are particularly wary and difficult to approach during the evening. While we would agree that this is true in the early evening, the reverse, in our experience, usually applies once the evening rise has commenced in earnest.

---

*These are traditional English fly patterns — *Editor.*

Our observations lead us to believe that the reason for the sudden transition from acute awareness to apparent unconcern, is less concerned with the trout's ability to see better than we can in most light. It is our belief that it is much more closely linked with the trout's focus and feeding behavior. That, and the fact that the light penetrating the surface and enabling the trout to see falls off sharply once the sun has set to the critical angle of 10 degrees to the water's surface.

Consider what happens. During the early part of the evening most trout take up lies in mid-water, and while a few individual fish may make odd forays to the surface to take the occasional dun or spinner floating down, the majority are merely observing, and waiting for the main hatch of dun or fall of spinner that normally occurs after the sun has set.

During this time, most trout are perhaps a couple of feet below the surface. At this depth, as already discussed, everything in the trout's window is in focus. What is more, because of the large aperture of his lens, also already noted, we know that in waning light he is likely to have better sight than the angler pursuing him. It is therefore not surprising that he is difficult to approach at this time: he can see well, because of his high-quality lenses; and all that he can see through his window is in focus.

As dusk approaches, however, the sequence of events discussed a page or so ago, sets in. The light reaching the fish gets rapidly less, and the fish moves closer and closer to the top, rising more frequently until, at the peak of the hatch, he is lying within a couple of inches of the surface. And the closer he moves to the surface, and the more he concentrates on it, the smaller his window gets and the more blurred distant objects in it become. And that includes the angler.

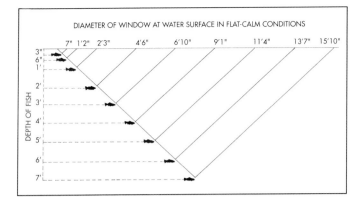

The diameters of the trout's window, as he nears and moves away from the surface. The figures are accurate to the nearest inch.

To facilitate an understanding of this sequence of events, and observations on the size of the window that we have made elsewhere in these chapters, we have compiled the illustration above. It shows the diameter of window of the trout at various depths; and how the size of the window diminishes as the fish moves upwards.

WHAT THE TROUT SEES OF THE FLY

From what has already been said, the surface of the trout's world can be likened to a large, bell-tent-shaped mirror facing downwards, except that, in the center, there is a circular area from which the silvering has been rubbed away.

This transparent circular area is the trout's window; and it is through this that he perceives the world above water. The window gets larger as he moves away from the surface, and smaller as he approaches it.

Let us now consider that most fascinating interrelationship: that between the trout and the surface fly.

The Fly on the Surface — and the "Triggers" to the Rise

Just as we cannot see through a mirror but only reflections *in* it, so it is with the trout. The trout can see nothing at all of the outside world through the mirror. In the area of the mirror, the only way that the trout can know that anything is present is where an object touches the surface film, or physically breaks through the surface film.

For this reason, when looking into the mirror, the trout can see the bodies of spent spinners and trapped terrestrial flies, *but not the bodies of most of the duns.*

The dead or dying spinner collapses spread-eagled onto the surface, its wings trapped in that cloying glue. Immediately, its body breaks through the surface film, and the instant it does so, it becomes visible to the trout.

The dun in the mirror, however, stands aloft *on* the surface film, and its abdomen is largely kept clear by the

Note the indentations that the feet of the advancing fly make in the mirror. Again, the trout cannot see through the mirror, and so cannot see the fly. But that starburst of light from the feet warns him that a fly is on its way. Who now, having seen fish rising in turbulent water, can believe the trout has less than perfect vision?

On the edge of the window, where he can see the fly as well.

legs and the natural upward arch of its body. The only means that the trout therefore has of spotting a distant dun floating on the mirror, is the tiny indentations that the fly's feet make in the surface film.

As shown clearly in these photographs (pages 100-101), the feet of the dun create tiny starbursts of light which the sharp eye of the trout can pick up from several feet away.

In the window, and as the fly assumes its familiar silhouette, the dimples of the feet become dark.

It is these starbursts of light created by the indentations of the feet of the dun floating on the surface, that are the first trigger to the trout's predatory mechanisms, and launch him on his way to the surface.

This trigger could be seen in action by large numbers of anglers if they were as concerned to observe a feeding trout and to learn from it, as they are to set about catching it at once. Time after time, a fish will be seen lying below the surface in a mid-water feeding position — and to begin to rise at a time when the laws of refraction as discussed earlier, make it clear the fish cannot see the body or wings of the approaching fly at all: they fall below the critical angle of 10 degrees that the trout needs to reach his eye before he can see anything of value.

If nothing that we have said hitherto has convinced the skeptic that the trout has the most remarkable eyesight, surely it is this: the fact that in rapid, broken water, the trout can pick out those tiny indentations in the surface film, and launch himself on an upward trajectory with deadly precision. (Indeed, it is probable that it is the indentations of the feet of the fly, when coupled with the trout's remarkable eyesight, that enable the fish in some cases to feed selectively. It is probable, in light of observations that we have made, that the trout is able to distinguish between the different indentations in the film, made by flies of markedly different size, when these are on the water at the same time.)

The starburst of light from the feet of the dun on the surface of the mirror (or, of course, the light refracted down from the struggles of a terrestrial fly or spinner) is not the only trigger that the trout's primitive predatory mechanisms have — although, in our opinion, it is by far the most important. There is a second trip-mechanism: the *wings* of the fly.

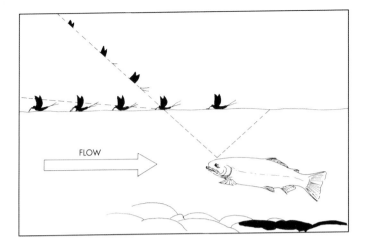

How the trout sees a dun approaching. The wings come into view first, "flared" over the edge of the window while the abdomen is still over the mirror. The abdomen itself does not come into view and join the disembodied wings until it also enters the window. It is only from the edge of the window onwards, that the trout can see the whole fly.

Consider a dun floating on the surface, in the mirror, towards the trout (or, if the trout is in a lake, consider a trout swimming towards the fly — the principle is exactly the same).

The fly, whose body is invisible to the fish, gradually gets nearer to the lowest rays of light which carry clear images of the outside world, down into the window of the trout. First the wings cut through those rays (see illustration above) and they appear, disembodied, up the "hill" on which everything the trout sees is positioned.

Gradually, more and more of the wings become visible as they cut through those lowest rays of "visible" light. Finally, as the body of the fly reaches the edge of the trout's

Here the bodies of the flies are in the mirror (note the double image of the fly on the right) . . . but the effects of refraction are already revealing the wings in the window of the trout.

window and itself is encompassed by the lowest rays, the body and wings *both* become visible, and the whole of the dun can be seen.

The speed of the process, of course, depends upon the rate of the current on the river, or the rate of approach of the trout in the lake; but in practice it happens smoothly and quite quickly, and the flaring effect of the wings from the position of the trout can be likened to a lighted, high-pressure gas jet: under full pressure, the flame appears some distance away from the aperture of the jet, but gradually, as the pressure is diminished, it gets nearer and nearer until it "joins" the jet itself.

The whole process of transition from the feet impressions in the mirror, to the flaring of the wings over the edge of the window, is made clear by the photographs on

The wings and the bodies are getting closer together, as the fly itself is carried towards the window.

pages 100 and 101 and these photographs on pages 104-106. It is largely because of this flaring effect that we believe that wings in floating flies (see later) can be helpful when addressing sophisticated trout.

Again, the confirming signal to the rising trout is the extraordinary flaring of the wings as they float, disembodied, over the rim of the window . . . eventually to join up with the abdomen. The wings begin to flare while the fly is still some distance away from the trout — as evidenced in the photograph on page 100.

Most trout do not wait for this second signal, but commit themselves from the moment they see the indentation of the feet.

Experienced trout, however, almost invariably do. They rise with great deliberation, and wings can sometimes mean the difference between failure and success.

The moment of union. The wings and the bodies come together on the edge of the window. In every case with these flies the bodies are visible throughout, because they have sunk into the surface. This is a common cause of failure with the traditionally dressed fly. Note how the new dressings that we have devised for the USD Paraduns, (see Appendix, pages 148-151), incorporate the triggers of both the feet and the wings, keeping the hook clear of the water.

Color in the Surface Fly

We have already established that the trout can see color, and have shown how the surface fly becomes visible to the fish from below water. Let us now draw these two together, and consider what the trout can see of the *color* of the surface fly.

The spent spinner, or any other fly whose body breaks through the surface film, is the most briefly summed up. As already discussed, the trout can see clearly anything that penetrates the mirror; and because he has excellent color vision, he can see the color of whatever has penetrated the mirror, as well. As a consequence, color in the body of the spent spinner and terrestrial flies is clearly of importance to the fly fisher.

The fly floating *on* the surface, however, is a much more complex proposition. Let us consider again the fly floating towards the trout, that we discussed a moment ago.

First of all, the fish sees the feet in the surface film. But under normal conditions the feet do not transmit color — simply sparkles of white light. The first that the trout sees of the fly itself is when the wing tips flare over the edge of his window. As the trout can see color, and can by definition see through his window, the color of the wings is therefore also a matter that the angler must consider. In the conventional artificial fly, as a consequence, the color of the *hackles* becomes particularly important because it is these which flare over the edge of the trout's window, in the manner of wings. It is, it should be noted, the hackles that are important even when a fly is tied with wings as well: the color of the hackle drowns the color of the wings, because the hackle reflects light more effectively.

As the body of the fly progresses from the mirror towards the window of the fish, it passes through the fine dividing line between the two — the prismatic ring known as Snell's Circle. For a brief moment in and beside that prismatic ring, when the sun is overhead or behind the trout, the whole color of the fly — wings *and* body — can be seen. Once through Snell's Circle, the fly passes further and further into the center of the window, becoming darker against the brilliant light overhead, as it goes. Most of this is made plain by the following photographs and accompanying illustrations.

For most fish, therefore, we are convinced that while the color of the hackle and/or wings on the dun *does* have importance, color in the body is of less consequence, and

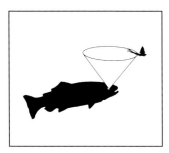
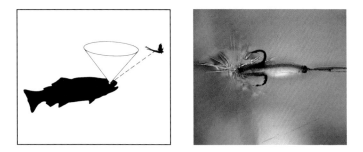

The first sight that the trout gets of the fly is when he sees it in the mirror as it approaches him (or, on stillwaters, as he swims towards it). If, as in the case above, the body of the fly penetrates the surface film, the fish can see the body color; otherwise all he can see is the feet of the fly, where they touch the surface. Note how the mirror's reflection shows the fish two hooks, not one.

The fly is now passing over the rim of the window (note sky appearing at the top). This is a photograph of profound importance to the angler. Most writers have argued that only size and shape are important in the artificial . . . that the fish sees only a silhouette in its window. In fact the full color of the artificial fly is visible to the trout: the fish has a narrow circle of full color vision around the edge of its window, whether or not the body of the fly penetrates the surface film . . . and many trout hold the fly in this circle, to study it more closely.

The fly begins to enter the window — and to lose its color. From this point on, color is less important. Even the body of the spinner, which lies in the surface film (unlike the dun, which stands on the surface film) loses color as it moves across the window.

Now the fly is directly overhead. At this point, the trout can see comparatively little color; the fly has become a near silhouette against the light. (Our comments above concern the appearance of the artificial against the light. Under some circumstances some natural flies become translucent when seen in the window).

the prime requirements of a successful floating fly — after the creation of suitable feet dimples — are correct size, silhouette and (to a certain degree) translucency.

Note, however, that we said for most fish and not for all fish. We believe that correct size and silhouette are the most important characteristics when fishing to the average trout, because the average trout is certainly not a very discriminating beast. Therefore, a well-dressed fly presented in a natural way to a steadily feeding fish will catch it nine times out of ten. The reason, we believe, is that the trout is programmed to recognize a series of generalities only — and when he sees them, *he reacts unless he has learned better.*

The average, inexperienced trout commits himself to the rise, in our experience, from the moment he sees the first of the generalities — the dimple patterns made by the feet in the mirror.

That is why the conventional fly works — it shows the trout what he wants or expects to see. In particular, it shows him the first of his two key trigger points: the hackles with which the fly is wound make light patterns in the surface film broadly similar to the light patterns made by the feet of the natural dun. As the trout therefore ascends to take the conventionally hackled fly, the trout has already "recognized" in it what he is looking for; and if he should pause briefly before consuming it, he will have his conviction reinforced: he will see its hackles flare over his window edge, for all the world like the wings he would also "expect" to see.

(It is an aside — but one worth mentioning — that there can be little doubt that many trout never really actually see the body of the fly that catches them, at all. If the fish is confident and unafraid, it will begin its rise as soon as the light dimples in the mirror are sighted. Then, if the trout's ascent is at the same rate as that at which the fly is approaching, its window will decrease in advance of the fly. The fly as a consequence will be "held" in the mirror, right up to the point at which it topples or is sucked into the mouth of the fish.)

Color and the Experienced Fish

And what of the experienced fish — the fish that has seen it all before; that is *not* content to commit its soul to a starburst of hackle points on the surface film? For this fish, we believe that everything has to be right, *including body color.*

Why body color? Let us go back again, to the fly floating towards an experienced trout on the current. The fish sees the indentations of the feet, and begins to rise to intercept. But not for him a mad, impulsive rush; he drifts up slowly and purposefully, in such a way as the fly, as he ascends, moves steadily from the mirror into his window. The

Color in the artificial fly can be important. An experienced fish will "lock on" to a fly when it enters the narrow area of close-up color vision that surrounds his window, and hold it there as he drops downstream with it. The distance at which a suspicious fish keeps the fly rarely seems to vary.

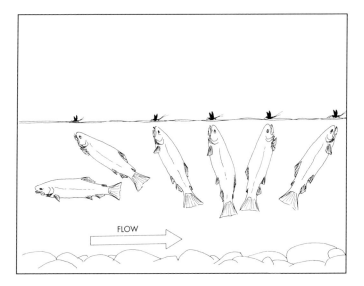

FLOW

111

wings begin to flare, and then to join up with the abdomen of the fly, on the very edge of his window.

In the normal course of events, the artificial fly would move quickly across the rim, and would darken swiftly into a silhouette against the light above. *But the wary, experienced fish, does not allow it to do so.* Indeed, why on earth should he? We have already discussed how the window is surrounded by a fine circular prism, and that it is only when the fly is in or very close to this, that the fish can see the color of the fly in all its detail.

When the sunlight is not behind the fly, to turn it into a silhouette the moment it appears, the experienced fish rises until the fly is on the edge of his window, and can be seen in full color. Then, the trout drops downstream with the fly, holding it there until he is satisfied that it is exactly what he wants. Only then will he rise. More commonly (it is why he has survived so long, and has become an experienced fish) he will not.

We have seen hundreds of experienced trout dropping downstream in this way, "locked on" to natural flies as well as artificials. The fly is held within an inch or two of the fish's nose, in fine focus, while the whole scrutiny process goes on.

We are quite sure that fish behaving in this way are using the full powers of vision and self-preservation that the good Lord has given them. Indeed, we do not believe it to be improbable that highly suspicious fish shift sufficiently below the fly to move it in and out of the window and prism, assessing in this way not simply color, but form as well and over and again in a single drift.

To meet the demands of these fish, we developed a range of duns and spinners which include USD Paraduns and Poly-Spinners which you'll find directions for tying in the Appendix, pages 147-154. They have been designed

A fly-dresser's portrait — the key features of the USD Dun.

A fly-dresser's portrait — the key features of the USD Poly-Spinner.

to give the experienced fish almost everything it could want: a body (in the dun's case) which stands aloft from the surface film; a body (in the spinner's case) which lies in the surface film; feet indentations in the mirror; wings to flare over the window's edge; appropriate color; accurate profile in the window; matching size.

How they compare (left to right): the conventional dun, the natural dun, and the USD Dun.

We do not believe that the hook is a great deterrent to the trout — and quite clearly to 99 trout out of a hundred it is no deterrent at all. In setting out to meet the requirements above, we found, nonetheless, that we had in some instances to remove the hook bend from the water to the air, and the trout do not seem to miss it much.

We have taken many fish of the kind just discussed, with such dressings. They are not infallible, any more than any artificial fly is likely to prove infallible (indeed, if an infallible fly *were* to be developed, millions would leave the sport after half a dozen outings; and the fish would go with them). The new dressings are, however, a most useful *supplement,* presenting the angler with a number of advantages over the conventional fly, when those advantages are most sorely needed: when he is confronted with difficult, experienced, desirable and often *large* trout, that turn up their imperious noses at wound-hackle flies. However, we feel we should point out that they are time-consuming patterns to dress, so we usually only use them very sparingly.

The spinner in the mirror. In the center, the natural fly; left, the conventional imitation; right, our new dressing, almost indistinguishable from Nature's model.

We would add one last point. Any trout will be made that much more difficult to catch if its suspicions are aroused. A careful, unobserved approach, and a delicate and accurate first cast, will do more to catch even an experienced fish than almost any refinement of the fly.

The same three flies (as pictured above) — and the same story — when viewed in the window . . . and note how starkly the hackles of the conventional dressing show up, when seen in silhouette.

Recognition of the Sub-Surface Fly

Away from the dazzling and brilliantly colored world of the surface, with its sunlight and its prisms, the world of the trout becomes a different place. The background is one of dull greens and browns and shadows and blurs; and the creatures which live there, and on which the trout feeds, are clad in similar hues.

In the greenish fastnesses of stillwater, the trout has no current to bring food to him; and so he must hunt it. In the hunting, he is obliged to rely a great deal on the movement and profile of his well-camouflaged prey, to help him to spot it.

One of the reasons that colored artificial wet flies attract so much more attention from trout on lakes is because the trout is better able to see color in a completely unadulterated way and — most importantly — because such flies are fished with *movement*.

On rivers, while the occasional fish will rummage his way among the stones and the gravel and the weeds, for the most part the trout is content to let the current bring his food to him. He hangs on the current, and relies on his powerful eyesight to help him to make quick judgments on what is and is not food, on the vast conveyor belt all around him.

In colored water and fast currents, the trout does not see any object until it is close up, and then he must make a quick decision on whether or not it is food. It seems likely, therefore, that his judgments under conditions such as these are based upon size, upon a quick impression of shape, and upon "life" as suggested by movement of legs and other appendages.

For trout in fast and colored water, therefore, precise imitation cannot be essential; and there can be little doubt, for example, that the North Country spider patterns* succeed not because they actually *look* like food, but because their soft, clinging hen hackles create in a hazy, impressionistic way, the qualities that the trout is hoping to see.

In the clearer and generally slower water of the chalkstreams and limestone rivers, the trout can see further, see more detail, and see it longer. Accurate representation is therefore much more important, and the most successful sub-surface patterns on clearwater streams are those that both *look* like the natural creature, and *behave* like the natural creature.

This, of course, is why some of the more popular weighted nymph, caddis pupae or cress bug patterns are so deadly. And that is why we believe there is enormous scope for the further imitation of the subaqueous food of river trout. (Precise imitation is by no means *always* necessary — and in addressing most fish we are inclined to functionalism in our nymphs. But there is, nevertheless, much interest and pleasure to be obtained from refinements in this field, by those prepared to seek it.)

Significance of the Mirror

As though the clearer and less turbulent water of the chalkstream and limestone river were not sufficient advantage, some trout which live in such comfortable surroundings have yet another aid to their subaqueous feeding: an aid shared only with the trout which hunt for nymphs, shrimps and their kin in the shallows of clear, calm lakes. They have the *mirror*.

We mentioned when discussing the optics of the underwater world in which the trout lives, that the mirror is

*These are wet-fly patterns which are very popular on English freestone rivers — *Authors*.

not like the ceiling of a vast room that recedes into the distance. It appears, instead, rather like the walls of a bell-tent that hang diagonally down around him. And because, as we said earlier, this optical effect places the mirror comfortably in front of him, it seems probable that in calm, shallow water the trout not only looks for the feet indentations of flies in the mirror, and their bodies trapped in it, as already discussed. Because the hanging screen of the mirror reflects everything on its underside, it seems highly likely that the trout addresses himself to it for reflections as well: for the movements of aquatic creatures wriggling their way up from the bottom, and along the bottom. By concentrating upon the mirror around or in front of him, the trout is able to see creatures that fall both above and below a line of concentrated vision directed elsewhere: in other words, the mirror provides him, in calm conditions, with a far wider range of view than it might at first be supposed he has.

For the river fisherman, who seldom finds himself on water free of surface distortion, such observations might appear interesting but not widely applicable. For the man who fishes lakes, however, there is a point to be made.

Because the mirror *is* a mirror, it reflects that side of any object or creature which is facing towards it. The mirror in a calm lake, therefore, reflects the *back* of any creature which is moving below it: and what is more, it reflects that back against the somber green-and-brown background of the reflected bottom. Nymphs for fishing shallow lakes in flat calm might therefore be designed with an awareness of this fact.

Because of the reflective properties of the mirror, and the likelihood that in calm water the trout uses the advantages it gives him when hunting nymphs and other sub-aqueous food, there seems to be an excellent case for

A photograph of great interest to the stillwater fisherman. In the center-bottom is an artificial nymph. In the center-top, a blob of white light glows in the mirror. What is the connection? The blob of light in the mirror is the reflection of a strip of silver we built into the back of the nymph. The reflection provides an unmistakable focus of attention for any trout using the mirror to help it find food — and could do so even if the nymph itself were lost in the weed, and was impossible to perceive by direct sight. (The "line" in the picture is simply a length of wire which we used to hold the nymph still while we took the photograph.)

incorporating into the dressings of some stillwater nymphs a tiny strip of white feather fiber or silver lurex,* mounted flat along the back.

Such a device would mean that the spot of light would be there, to attract attention against the dark background of the mirror — but size, profile and general coloration would be preserved, and would aid deception when the nymph is addressed by the trout with direct vision.

WHAT THE TROUT SEES OF THE ANGLER

In addition to our observations of the fly as perceived from below water we also, using a range of specially constructed observation tanks, and cameras sunk into the riverbed, carried out a series of underwater experiments designed to throw practical light on matters of day-to-day consequence to the fly fisher.

The observation tanks we used were set up carefully to reproduce natural underwater conditions found in the wild including (and most important of all for our observation and photographic purposes) *natural intensities of light*. The cameras we sank into the riverbed were mounted in wholly natural stretches of water, unadulterated in any way. We will address our experiments and observations one by one; and where we believe it permissible we will draw conclusions from the results.

Visibility of the Angler

Notwithstanding the theoretical position concerning underwater illumination (it is that a proportion of even the lowest rays of light go down to the eye of the trout, with that proportion getting less and less as the rays get nearer

---

*In American usage, mylar — *Editor*.

the horizontal), we wanted to discover what the practical effect is on the angler of this fall off in penetration.

To test the true effect, we constructed a pole six feet in height, with cross pieces; and painted it with different colors of fluorescent paint (for visibility) at measured intervals down its face. We then positioned this somewhat gaudy "angler" at water level, at various distances from the edge of the window as perceived by an observer below water level.

As our "angler" was moved further and further away from the observer, a note was made of the lowest point on him which retained a meaningful shape. The angle between that lowest point, and the plane of the water surface, was then measured at each movement, with a theodolite.*

At once, we made an important discovery. Although, thanks to the unnatural intensity of the colors with which the pole had been painted, we could actually see a trace of the lower part of the pole to a height corresponding to an angle of 1.9 degrees from the water surface, this trace visibility was of no practical use. The lowest light rays were so dull, so sharply refracted, and so compressed on the outside of the window (a point depicted in the illustrations on pages 84 and 85) that nothing sensible could actually be *seen.*

It was only at an angle of 9.8 degrees to the water surface that parts of the angler became reasonably visible. It is for this reason that in our diagrams concerning the angle of penetration of light, and in our discussion surrounding them, that we discounted rays entering the water at less than 10 degrees to the horizontal. We are fully aware that

---

*A surveying tool used to measure horizontal and vertical angles — *Editor.*

How a wading angler appears to the trout — and a theory disproved. Ever since angling writers have begun to investigate trout vision, it has been believed that the trout approached by a wading angler must see four legs — the real legs, and their reflection in the mirror. This picture was one of several dozens we took with a camera sunk into the bed of the river. No legs at all were visible in any of our pictures even though (as in the photograph here) Brian Clarke approached to within seven feet of the camera in water that was crystal clear in any fishing sense. The reason why no legs show is, we believe, one of the by-products of the curious optical effect of "the sloping mirror" discussed on page 87.

some penetration *does* occur below that level, but this is of little practical value to the trout under typical or normal circumstances.

From a typical surface feeding position of 12 inches below the film, the practical effect of a 10-degree angle was that the angler was clearly visible from a little below the waist up — and then, of course, very much foreshortened — at a distance of five yards. At 10 yards, only the head and top of his shoulders could clearly be seen.

There is, however, one important proviso that we would add to all of this. Any sudden movement below 10 degrees by a bright object could be seen at almost every point down the angler's "body" — even down as far as the 1.9 degree line, below which all vision was lost.

This finding clearly has some significance in the approach to the trout. While the trout is unlikely to see anything below the level of the angler's knees even when he is close up, it *does* argue even for careful movement of the hands, when working against a dark background in conditions of bright sun and flat calm.

The river angler is unlikely to find many fly-fishing stretches where the water surface is truly flat. The still-water trout fisherman is, however, particularly on the smaller, man-made lakes.

The Rod and Clothing

We conducted a number of tests using gloss-varnished and matt-varnished rods in conditions of bright sunlight, at different distances from the window. In every case, when a gloss-varnished rod (particularly a flat-sided split-cane rod) caught the sunlight, it heliographed its presence to the observer below water, almost regardless of its position. This, of course, was very much what we had expected to find, when taken in conjunction with our discoveries concerning movement set out in the paragraphs above.

It seems to us to provide a strong argument for the abandonment of the current practice of gloss-varnishing rods, and for matt-varnishing them, instead. There can be no knowing how many fish are not caught not because they have been "spooked", but simply because they have been put "on guard" by something as simple as the flash from a highly varnished rod, even when it is being carried

Rod flash shows clearly in the above photograph. It is quite clear that the reflection of bright sunlight off gloss varnish must alert many trout, whether or not the angler is aware of it at the time.

low-down by the angler. In all of our experiments concerning the reflecting powers of rods, the matt-varnished rod was much less easily seen.

In addition to the matter of reflection, we tested the visibility of rods at different angles to the surface, at different distances from the observer.

When held vertically, close to the traditional casting position, even the thinnest rod at five yards distant became grossly thickened by the effects of refraction: indeed, a seven-and-a-half foot wand at five yards distant took on the appearance of a thick billiard cue, when held vertically. A similar — though less obtrusive — thickening occurred when the rod was 10 yards distant.

In both cases, we found that the rod became less and less visible as it was dropped from the vertical to the horizontal; and that once below 45 degrees from the vertical, it all but disappeared.

This observation seems to us to provide the best possible case for preferring the horizontal cast to the vertical cast, even though in many circumstances it can be incredibly difficult to perform. This observation must be of particu-

Why the horizontal cast should be preferred to the vertical. In this photograph, taken when the anglers were seven yards distant, the horizontal rod is almost invisible, while the vertical rod looms into the window of the trout. The vertical rod always appears to thicken, when viewed through the window.

lar importance when the fly fisherman is wading in broad shallows, and fishing the open margins of rivers and lakes.

As a last test of the visibility of the fly fishermen and all of his accoutrements, we viewed fly fishermen dressed in a variety of colors, against a typical range of fishing backgrounds. As we expected, the clothing which best matched the surrounding background was the one that was the least visible from below water. The most visible colors, regardless of where they were positioned, were — without question — red, orange and yellow.

Fly Lines

One of the most vexed questions about angling equipment is that concerning the best color of fly line for use in surface fishing. We decided to examine this subject in some detail, in an attempt to discover the truth.

All the debate that we have seen on this issue has concerned the color of fly lines both in the air and on the water, in the window of the fish. We therefore set up

How a green and a white line in the air, appear to the trout through his window. While the darker line is in the main more easily seen, the score is evened-up by the occasional flash the white line gives off (note lower-right of the picture).

experiments that would allow us to observe white, brown and green lines, in each of these positions.

In the first instance, we cast the three lines at various distances *above* the water surface, across the window. At every level, the green and brown lines were more visible than the white fly line against the sky above. Towards the outside edge of the window, where there was a background of trees, the white line showed up marginally more clearly. In both cases, however, the white fly line showed one tendency that the others did not: in bright sunlight it gave off an occasional flash that was clearly

This photograph reveals the truth . . . that it is not the line in the air or in the window that should be considered, but the line on the water in the mirror. The white fly line, although it causes a degree of flash (right) in the air, is most of the time less visible to the trout. But it falls like a flash of white lightning across all the water surrounding the trout . . . across the mirror. There can be little doubt, as a consequence of our experiments and photographs such as the one above, that white or light-colored fly lines should not be used when the trout are close to the surface.

visible below water. In the air, therefore, it seemed that the balance between the lines was finely placed, with the white line probably having the edge.

On the water in the window, the argument that the white fly line would be less visible to the trout when viewed against the light of the sky above, was proved fallacious. The white fly line *cut off* the light reaching the observer's position below water quite as effectively as the green and brown lines; and reflected light from the bottom, while slightly illuminating the underside of the white fly line, did not make any difference of practical account. Once again, therefore, we came to the conclusion that there was little to choose between the colors.

Then we decided to conduct a different experiment: an experiment to explore a point not yet raised in the public debate, and going beyond the visibility of the line in the air, and the line on the water, in the window.

We tested the three lines in the mirror.

The results of this experiment produced one of the most startling moments that we have experienced in the years in which we have been carrying out our research.

We viewed the brown, green and white fly lines lying in the mirror, when it was reflecting a bottom of (a) gravel and rocks, (b) weed, and (c) chalk and weed.

In every case, the white fly line was vastly more visible than the green or brown lines. It lay like a bright crack in the face of the mirror; and when cast onto the mirror, it fell like a flash of lightning across the whole field of view.

This experiment proved that a white, yellow or peach fly line can be a significant handicap on rivers, even when the angler knows where his fish is: he can keep the bright line away from his target trout — but he is likely to spook more violently any unseen fish in the vicinity of the line where it falls on the water. And those unseen fish, when spooked, are likely to disturb the trout that he wants.

This is even more important to the angler fishing stillwaters, however, than it is to the angler fishing in shallow streams for trout that he can see by rise-form. The

Casting dry flies on the Fall River, California. ➤

stillwater angler rarely knows the exact position of his trout; and more often casts without knowing how many fish are within his casting range, or where they are.

For the stillwater angler, it seems certain that the flash of white lightning across most of the surface field of view of any trout in the vicinity will startle or put on guard his quarry, and so will much reduce his chances of success. The only alleviating factor that can be employed by the man who uses light fly lines on stillwaters in calm conditions, is a very long leader: it will enable him to put a greater distance between his fly or nymph and the "area of shock". In other words it will allow him partly to offset the disadvantage he has given himself.

We say this notwithstanding the fact that we have both used light-colored lines (although, let us add, almost always in conjunction with long leaders) on stillwater hitherto. The fact is that, as a consequence of our experiments, we now know better their disadvantages.

We have also shown that any discussion of fly lines against the light whether in the air or on the surface, is largely irrelevant. It is the *mirror* that counts, every time.

Leaders

We tested three leaders of equal diameter, one greased with a floatant, one treated to sink by applying to it a compound of glycerine and fuller's earth,* and one not treated at all, but wiped clean with a soft, dry cloth. The greased leader came off worst in both the window and the mirror. Refraction around the edges of the floatant made it appear to "thicken" over and above the added width of the floatant itself. The leader that was simply wiped clean was conspicuous in the surface film at every point, but

---

* A highly absorbent claylike substance — *Editor.*

Why — even when fishing the surface fly — the leader should never be greased close to its end. Of the three leaders shown, the least visible is the center one, treated to sink. The leader on the left was simply wiped clean. The leader on the right was dressed with a floatant.

was less easily seen below the surface. The leader treated to sink was, because of its opaque dressing, more easy to see below the surface than the wiped leader but, of course, it had the advantage of not appearing on the surface at all. In view of this, and the results of our drag observations recorded below, we had reinforced our faith in a leader treated to sink throughout the last few feet of its length, where fishing conditions and technique allow.

Drag

It is easy to understand, once it has been seen from the position of the trout, why drag can kill the angler's chances dead.

In addition to observing the appearance of stationary leaders in the mirror and the window, we observed leaders being drawn across the surface at different speeds.

We found that drag creates enormous visual disturbance when viewed from below; and that, perhaps not
surprisingly, the degree of disturbance was proportional
to the rate of movement. Anything other than the very
slowest rates of retrieve set up a continuing series of thin
fish bone ripples in the surface film, either side of the
leader. Against the light, these fish bone crinkles flashed
alternately light and dark, with the most pronounced
visual effect occurring exactly where the angler would not
wish it — on the edge of the window.

In each of these tests, the leader treated to float created
worse drag than the leader that had simply been wiped
clean. Again, the lesson seemed obvious; keep grease
away from the end of your leader near your fly — *particularly* when fishing dry.

Sunset and the Dry Fly

Various experiments that we conducted to discover
how the appearance of a given fly might vary as the sun
moved on its normal course during a day's time, resulted
in one absorbing and fascinating observation made with
the spinner, at sunset.

Brian Clarke had long believed that the effectiveness of
the Orange Quill* and similarly colored dry flies de-
pended largely upon their position in relation to the sun,
when perceived by the trout. In particular, he believed
that the reason they succeeded *when* they succeeded (in
the evening) was because the low red rays of the setting
sun reflected off the wings of the natural fly, down to the
trout below: in other words, that sunlight on the wings of
the fly, changed the fly's color.

---

*This is a very old and popular English pattern that was
so beloved by Skues — *Authors.*

He had already observed that the wings of the natural spinner, when held in a position to reflect the light, acted very much like cats' eyes at night. The cross-work of veins broke up the brilliance of the spinner's wings into a great number of highly reflective facets — and the rays of the setting sun on these facets changed the color of the wings to a variety of shades between pale pink and bright orange.

It was in setting up an experiment to test this theory underwater that our surprise observation was made.

First of all, we found the theory concerning the upright wings to be partly proven: they did indeed take on a pink glow when viewed in the window from below water, when at an appropriate angle to the sun. The glow was not, however, as strong as we had expected that it would be.

Far more interesting was a phenomenon we had not even suspected — the effect of light from the red setting sun on the feet dimples of the dun *when seen in the mirror;* and its effect on the *spread-eagled wings* of the spinner, when similarly viewed.

In the case of the feet, instead of making a few sparkles of light like white diamonds, the indentations in the surface film took on the appearance of brilliant rubies against the somber background of the mirror at dusk.

In the case of the spent spinner, the fly was utterly transformed.

The wings of the spent spinner always trap air beneath the corrugated patchwork of veins mentioned above; and the appearance of this trapped air in the mirror, under conditions of normal daylight, is rather like a piece of veined bathroom window surrounded by a white halo.

In a red sunset, when viewed from certain positions below water, all of this white light glows gold or red: the fly appears to glow like soft fire (see photograph on the next page).

Herein, we believe, lies one of the answers to the age-old problem of the difficult evening rise.

It seems very likely that as the light gets worse, the trout, consequently, begins to eat only those flies he can most easily see — and science has already established that the color the trout sees most easily in freshwater is . . . *red.*

If this is indeed the case it seems probable that when there is a colorful sunset, a fly with an orange hackle will

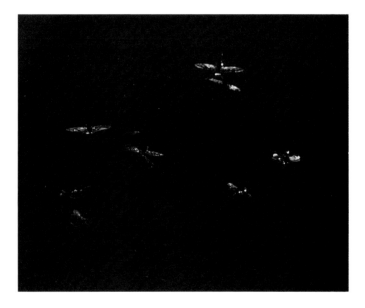

How does the trout see flies in the dusk, when the angler cannot see them at all? These spinners, drifting over the camera like silent, eerie moonships, provide the answer. Although the fly may be invisible from above water, the last rays of light are refracted down from around its body and make it clearly visible when viewed from below water, against the somber background of the mirror. Some refraction occurs while even the merest amount of light remains.

attract the attention of more trout than will an accurate representation of the natural fly as the angler sees it.

Our observation concerning the effect of evening light on spinners' wings and duns' feet in the mirror was made as the draft of this book was going to press. As a consequence, we have not had the opportunity to test our conclusion under field conditions. Nevertheless, we confidently expect a positive response from the fish, when we do.

OVERLEAF: *Trout fishing on Armstrong Spring Creek, Montana.*

POSTSCRIPT

At the time of writing this note it is one year since *The Trout and the Fly* was published, and although a second reprint has intervened, this third reprint is the first opportunity we have had to make any addition at all. In the tiny amount of space that has been made available to us, we want to add, very briefly, a few points which have emerged in that year, in discussions between ourselves as we have continued to observe and experiment.

The following points are listed in random order, with the exception of the first, which is of transcendent importance.

1) The importance of the mirror to the trout (and so to the angler) cannot be overstated. It will emerge and re-emerge through the points which follow. Although the window has been the subject of far more discussion in angling literature, we believe that its importance pales beside that of the mirror, for a trout feeding at the surface. Once the significance of this is grasped, it opens up a new dimension for fly fisher and fly dresser alike. The mirror has been the forgotten frontier of the angler's world.

2) Trout which are feeding at the surface appear to the angler to lie level in the water, looking ahead of them, when they are waiting (on a river) for a fly to come into view. There is an implicit assumption in this that if the trout is lying horizontally, it must have its eyes cocked

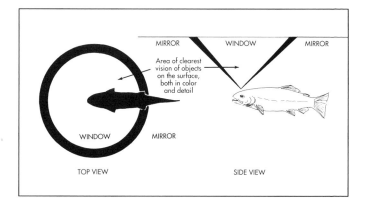

MIRROR   WINDOW   MIRROR

Area of clearest
vision of objects
on the surface,
both in color
and detail

WINDOW   MIRROR

TOP VIEW   SIDE VIEW

upwards, looking at the surface some distance ahead. We believe this may well not be the case. Instead, we believe that a trout on the lookout for surface food approaching from the mirror may lie at an angle to the surface, with the angle of tilt varying in accordance with the distance ahead and overhead on which the fish is concentrating.

Our observations in the field have appeared to confirm the validity of this belief. However, it can be theorized about as well, for those who prefer meat on the bone.

We will consider the two extreme stages: the angle at which the fish's body is inclined when it takes the fly, and the angle from which it might start off on its ascent.

The first is the easier to deal with. We have photographed many trout which have broken the surface with their nebs* at the moment of taking the fly. Without exception, these photographs have shown the neb of the fish pointing into the air at a very steep angle to the surface, while the body of the fish below water appears to lie at the shallow angle to the surface at which the angler is used to seeing it. The series of photographs on the next

*In American usage, noses or snouts — *Editor.*

pages illustrate the point perfectly — and the difference between the real angle indicated by the head of the fish, and the apparent angle of the body in the water, must obviously be accounted for by refraction.

A small heavily weeded trout stream that is never stocked . . . and Brian Clarke sees a wild brown tight in to the bank. It rises to take a small dark fly. It looks huge . . .

The fly alights and drifts over the big trout's nose. Time stands still and years of experience go into the assessment . . . The trout wonders is that fly REAL?

Yes . . . The mouth slowly begins to open although the trout is not yet fully committed.

The moment of decision for the trout . . . a slight adjustment of the fins, a tilt to the water's surface, and the huge mouth opens in an utterly confident take.

Deceived! The leader tightens, and the camera freezes the instant of Truth. Note the alarm in the fish's eye. What is it?

The evidence for the fish being angled even before he begins his ascent, in spite of appearances, is circumstantial but interesting — with again, of course, any difference between actual angle and perceived horizontal position again being accounted for by refraction.

While a trout can see with one eye, it can judge distances only by looking with both eyes. The trout focuses by moving its lens towards and away from its retina. Because the lens is dependent for movement on a ligament which cannot retract but whose position is known, and a muscle which can retract and the position of which is also known, the direction of travel of the lens towards the retina can be established. This direction, we understand, is consistent with the fish receiving its clearest image towards the back of the retina: the direction in which the image would apparently be transmitted through the lens if the fish were looking forwards.

For a fish to look directly forward with both eyes at an object or area, it must point its body in the direction it wishes to look; it just doesn't have a neck to enable it to do anything else. And if that object or area is the water surface, the fish presumably must point its body towards the surface: in other words, it seems it must lie with its body angled upwards, towards the surface, when on the lookout for surface food.

3) We have already mentioned that at least in many cases, a fish is inclined at a very steep angle when it accepts a fly from the water surface. We do not know exactly what this angle is, but it is interesting to speculate. We suspect that it is of the order of 50 degrees to the vertical. We believe this to be the case because we already know that the fish gets its clearest and most detailed view of the fly insofar as light is concerned, when the fly is just on the inside edge of the window. And we also already know that he will get his best view insofar as his eyes are concerned by looking straight ahead with both eyes.

As interception of a surface fly calls for fine judgment, we believe that the trout will instinctively make use of every facility available to him — through both light and eye. In other words, in the final stages of the rise it is probable that he looks at the edge of his window with both eyes looking directly forward: and he can do that only by pointing his head and body at it. Light comes to his eye from the edge of his window at around 48 degrees to the vertical and it therefore seems probable that he aligns his body roughly along this path.

4) The mirror at night is pitch dark. We have shown through our photographs just how easily the trout can see the spinner at sunset and in moonlight, when looking up towards the mirror — even though that same fly is invisible to the angler looking down. What happens is that the

spread-eagled, transparent wings of the fly allow what light there is to pass through them — and so they appear as small pools of light in the otherwise total darkness of the mirror all around.

Extending the same principle to fly lines, a floating line of any kind or color is visible to the fish at night if that line is lying in the surface film and is moved. It refracts some light down from around its sides, and any disturbance the line makes is clearly evident. (It is also true that at night the lighter in color a line is, the more noticeable it is, whether moved or not.)

There are several implications in all of this. A number of writers have noted that sea trout being fished for at night become more difficult to catch when the moon is behind the angler: the reason, they have said, is because the silhouetted angler casts shadows down the pool into the window of the trout. This may indeed be the case. But we believe it just as likely that the fish are difficult to catch for a different or supplementary reason. If the moon is behind the angler from the position of the fish, then it is behind the line as well. And if the line is on the surface and moved, then it will create an alarming herringbone light pattern in the darkness of the mirror that the trout or sea trout can see.

5) Nylon floating on the surface allows light — much after the manner of spread-eagled spinners' wings — to pass through it. If clear nylon is used on the surface at night, the light passing through it will appear like a bright crack in the darkness of the mirror: a crack which runs right up to any surface fly being fished! There are obvious lessons in this not just for the fly fisher (keep your leader as well-sunk at night as you do during the day) — but for the coarse angler as well — particularly for anglers who free line floating bread to carp at night.

6) We have carried out exhaustive tests on different-colored leaders on and below the surface in conditions ranging from noonday sun to dark night. While the ideal leader will obviously be one dyed to the color the mirror is reflecting from the bottom over any given area of bed, we have found that a leader dyed brown is the least obtrusive over the widest range of conditions. A black leader, as might be expected, is least visible against the mirror at night. Again, all leaders are less visible below the surface at night, just as they are during the day — again something it might be helpful for carp anglers and others to note.

7) It has nothing to do with refraction, but trout in chalkstreams cannot see nearly as far as some fly fishers would believe. The water looks gin-clear when illuminated by the sun, and viewed from above. But the trout must look horizontally through the water, and all the billions of particles of suspended chalk reflect light back to him. The effect, as we have seen demonstrated by a cine-camera sunk into the riverbed, and pointed horizontally, is very much like switching on one's car headlights in a fog. Under some circumstances, chalkstream trout cannot see more than two or three feet. Under many circumstances, chalkstream trout cannot see more than four or five feet. Even in the clearest and shallowest chalkstream, under the most favorable light conditions, it is doubtful if the fish can see 10 feet through the water. These observations are not, of course, valid for trout in clear lakes, wherein there is no flow to disturb and carry sediment. Nor do we believe it invalidates the photograph and caption of Brian Clarke on page 122: that photograph was taken in water which was scarcely moving.

8) The dressings of the USD dun and spinner were designed to reproduce as near-exactly as possible the

precise optical effects presented to the trout by natural flies. However, we have found through further experimentation that the hooking properties of the dun can be improved by replacing the cut-hackle wings with a few calftail fibers; and the hooking properties of the spinners can be improved by tying them exactly as described but on standard hooks for broken water; and on standard hooks without any parachute hackle at all, on smooth water. Dressed in this last way, where it can be fished, this spinner dressing is deadly.

Brian Clarke
John Goddard
February, 1981

Overleaf: *Ray Grubb on a private spring creek.*

APPENDIX

HOW TO TIE THE USD PARADUNS AND
THE USD POLY-SPINNERS

Authors' Note: We developed all of our patterns as a result of our own observations and experiments. After the first reprint of *The Trout and the Fly*, however, it was drawn to our attention that at least two other anglers — some time before us — had arrived at a dressing of an upside-down dun which was similar (though not identical) to the one we devised. As they were faced with the same problems of optics and aerodynamics, and the range of possible solutions to these problems (once they are understood) is somewhat limited, perhaps this is not surprising. We want to give credit, therefore, at this, our first opportunity, to those anglers who preceded us. The first we understand to have been one John Slotherton, who wrote about his version of a USD fly in the *Journal of Flyfishers' Club* (London) in the early months of 1933. Slotherton's dressing was picked up and repeated subsequently in books by Colonel Joscelyn Lane, but Slotherton was the designer. The second angler to have arrived at a similar dressing was Hal Janssen, who apparently published the results of his work (a pattern called "The Stalker") in a magazine article published in the United States some time in 1973.

USD PARADUN

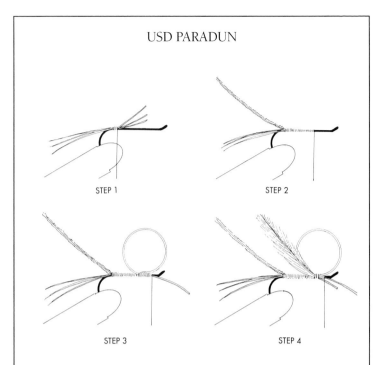

Step 1) Take a thread along the shank and well around the bend. Secure two or three whisks or a bunch of hackle fibers, as appropriate.

Step 2) Secure the body material at the bend of the hook, and then take the thread two-thirds of the distance back to the hook's eye.

Step 3) Next, tie in a loop of nylon. Be careful not to pull the loop too tight.

Step 4) Secure a good quality, short-flue hackle at right angles to the shank, as close to the bend side of the loop as possible. Trim off butt.

Step 5) Cut the wings from near the top center of a good quality hen hackle using a wing cutter. (*Not illustrated*)

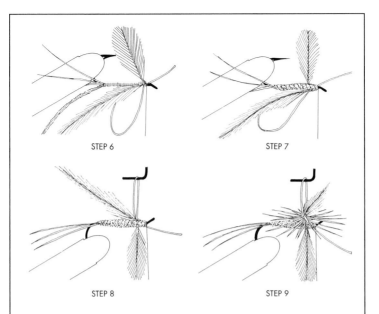

STEP 6 STEP 7

STEP 8 STEP 9

Step 6) Reverse hook in vice (and for pattern with rib, see step 7). With figure-of-eight tying, secure a pair of cut wings in such a way that they appear as a V when viewed from eye of the hook. Cut off the two butts, and then run a dubbing needle up the outside of both wings under a little pressure, to give them a pronounced outward curve.

Step 7) Wind the body material up to the eye, and trim off the excess. (Note: if a pattern with a rib is being dressed, this operation will have to be carried out before the wings are tied in.)

Step 8) Reverse the hook in the vice. Take the loop of nylon onto a gallows tool, and prepare to put two to four turns of the hackle as tightly and as low as possible around the loop.

Step 9) Take the turns of hackle around the loop. Pass the tip through the loop, hold with the finger and thumbs and begin to draw loop tight.

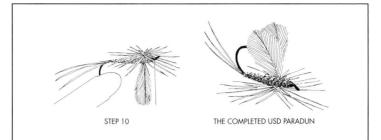

STEP 10 THE COMPLETED USD PARADUN

Step 10) The loop is now pulled tight to trap the hackle point, and the excess hackle is trimmed. Now apply a blob of varnish where the center of the hackle is trapped under the loop. When the varnish is dry, trim off any excess nylon from the loop, and remove any hackle fibers projecting below the horizontal.

Dressings

No. 1 USD Para-Blue Winged Olive
Thread: Orange
Hook: 12, 14 or 16 UE
Tails: Three muskrat or mink whiskers, colored dark olive, or bunch of hackle fibers
Body: Natural heron hurl
Wings: Dark gray or dark blue dun
Hackle: Rusty dun

No. 2 USD Para-Olive
Thread: Brown
Hook: 12, 14 or 16 UE
Tails: Two muskrat or mink whiskers, colored olive, or bunch of hackle fibers
Body: Heron hurl dyed olive in picric acid
Wings: Pale blue dun
Hackle: Olive cock

No. 3 USD Para-Pale Watery
Thread: Yellow
Hook: 16 or 17 UE
Tails: Bunch of pale honey hackle fibers
Body: Grayish goose primary herls
Wings: Cream or pale blue dun
Hackle: Rusty dun

USD SPINNER

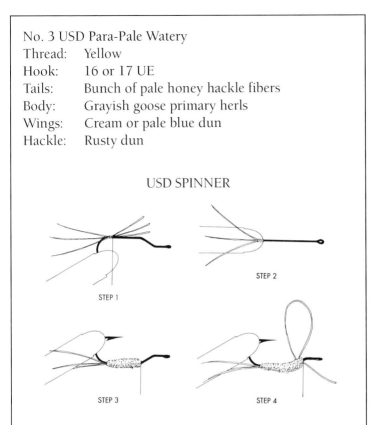

STEP 1

STEP 2

STEP 3

STEP 4

Step 1)   Wind the thread down to the bend, and tie in two or three mink whiskers for the tails.

Step 2)   The tails should be spread well apart, as shown above. A blob of varnish applied to the base, will hold them in position.

Step 3)   Reverse the hook. Dub the body material onto the thread, and wind along the shank to the keel's end.

Step 4)   Tie in the loop of nylon (not too tightly) halfway up the slope from the keel to the eye. Dub a little more body material onto the thread, and take a fraction further towards the eye.

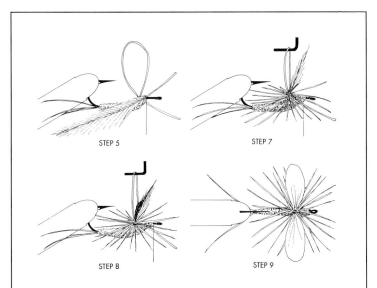

STEP 5

STEP 7

STEP 8

STEP 9

Step 5) Tie in the hackle by the butt, as close as possible to the base of the loop. Then fit the gallows tool to the vice.

Step 6) Cut the wings from a doubled sheet of the lightest gauge polyethylene utilizing one of the new cutters in the appropriate size, and then pierce with a blunt needle. (The wings should be prepared beforehand.) (*Not illustrated*)

Step 7) According to hook size, take between two and five turns of hackle tightly around the base of the loop, and then pass the tip through the loop. Hold the tip with finger and thumb until step 8 has been completed.

Step 8) Pass the pre-cut, thin-gauge polyethylene wings through the loop.

Step 9) Pull nylon tight to secure both hackle-point and wings. Give wings extra security by binding with a figure-of-eight tying. (This is not an easy operation to perform, as the thread at each cross-over must be woven in between the hackle fibers, without trapping any of them.) Finish head with whip finish, and varnish.

Dressings

No. 1 USD Poly-Pheasant-Tail Spinner
Thread: Orange
Hook: 12 or 14 keel hooks
Tails: Two muskrat or mink whiskers, colored pale
         brown
Body: Pheasant-tail fiber
Wings: Polyethylene, cut with wing cutter
Hackle: Rusty dun cock

No. 2 USD Poly-Red Spinner
Thread: Brown
Hook: 12, 14 or 16 keel hooks
Tails: Two muskrat or mink whiskers, colored
         pale blue
Body: Red seal's fur
Wings: Polyethylene, cut with wing cutter
Hackle: Pale blue dun cock

No. 3 USD Poly-Yellow Boy Spinner
Thread: Yellow
Hook: 14 or 16 keel hooks
Tails: Two muskrat or mink whiskers, colored pale
         yellow
Body: Medium yellow seal's fur
Wings: Polyethylene, cut with wing cutter
Hackle: Light buff cock

No. 4 USD Poly-Orange Spinner

Thread:	Orange
Hook:	14 keel hook
Tails:	Three muskrat or mink whiskers, colored brown
Body:	Orange seal's fur
Rib:	DFM orange floss
Wings:	Polyethylene, cut with wing cutter
Hackle:	Bright ginger cock

No. 5 USD Sherry Spinner
(Skues Type)

Thread:	Orange
Hook:	14 keel hook
Tails:	Three muskrat or mink whiskers, colored pale brown
Body:	Orange and green seal's fur mixed with fur from a hare's poll
Rib:	Fine gold wire
Wings:	Polyethylene, cut with wing cutter
Hackle:	Pale honey dun cock with dark center

INDEX